Featuring Essays by

Keegan-Michael Key
Lynda Lopez
Jennine Capó Crucet
Andrea González-Ramírez
Patricia Reynoso
Pedro A. Regalado
Rebecca Traister
Natalia Sylvester
Erin Aubry Kaplan
Tracey Ross
Carmen Rita Wong
Mariana Atencio
Wendy Carrillo
Nathan J. Robinson
Prisca Dorcas Mojica Rodriguez
Elizabeth C. Yeampierre
María Cristina (MC) González Noguera

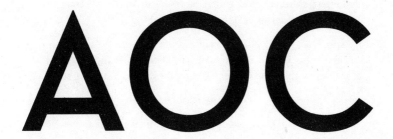

AOC

The Fearless Rise and
Powerful Resonance of
ALEXANDRIA OCASIO-CORTEZ

Edited by
LYNDA LOPEZ

ST. MARTIN'S
PRESS
NEW YORK

First published in the United States by St. Martin's Press,
an imprint of St. Martin's Publishing Group

www.stmartins.com

Designed by Steven Seighman

"An Open Letter to Congresswoman Ocasio-Cortez" © Jennine Capó
Crucet; "The Imagined Threat of a Woman Who Governs Like a Man" by
Rebecca Traister originally appeared in *The Cut* on September 19, 2018; a
version of "In No Uncertain Terms" by Natalia Sylvester originally
appeared in the *New York Times* on September 20, 2019; "On Being an
Indignant Brown Girl" © Prisca Dorcas Mojica Rodriguez

Library of Congress Cataloging-in-Publication Data

Names: Lopez, Lynda, 1971- editor.
Title: AOC: the fearless rise and powerful resonance of Alexandria
   Ocasio-Cortez / edited by Lynda Lopez.
Other titles: Alexandria Ocasio-Cortez
Description: First edition. | New York : St. Martin's Press, 2020.
Identifiers: LCCN 2020005577 | ISBN 9781250257413 (hardcover) |
   ISBN 9781250257406 (ebook)
Subjects: LCSH: Ocasio-Cortez, Alexandria, 1989—Influence. | United
   States. Congress. House—Biography. | Hispanic American women
   legislators—Biography. | Legislators—United States—Biography. |
   Hispanic American women—Political activity. | Hispanic
   Americans—Political activity. | New York (N.Y.)—Biography.
Classification: LCC E901.1.O27 A55 2020 | DDC 328.73/092 [B]—dc23
LC record available at https://lccn.loc.gov/2020005577

Our books may be purchased in bulk for promotional, educational, or
business use. Please contact your local bookseller or the Macmillan
Corporate and Premium Sales Department at 1-800-221-7945, extension
5442, or by email at MacmillanSpecialMarkets@macmillan.com.

First Edition: 2020

10 9 8 7 6 5 4 3 2

To my mother, Guadalupe, and my sisters Leslie and Jennifer—the original fearless Latinas who taught me anything was possible . . .
And to my little one, Lucie—the reason I do everything.

Contents

Preface

Keegan-Michael Key

My wife and I were sitting in bed one evening, scrolling through social media, and came across a video of Alexandria Ocasio-Cortez fearlessly dismantling an ill-prepared Mark Zuckerberg before Congress. Elle and I looked at each other and both had the same excited thought; AOC don't play.

There are many things that I admire about Alexandria Ocasio-Cortez, including her drive and ambition, her fearless tenacity, and her seemingly boundless energy to fight for us all. She has become a voice, not only for the Latina contingency in this nation, but for the youth, the disenfranchised, the economic underclass, and those who have a desire to exercise moral courage. I am honored to write this Preface and am grateful that there is now a Latina policy-making millennial forging a new path in politics. This book is an homage to her and those she inspires.

On many issues that we are currently facing in this country I understand AOC's perspective. I grew up in a lower-middle class home near 8 Mile in Detroit. I had a fairly traditional, middle-American church-going up-bringing. We didn't know what bootstraps were. But we learned it's important to pay taxes; in order for our roads to be paved, so we can drive safely and efficiently to our jobs, where we're paid a wage that was legislated by a government body for our financial welfare, and in a work environment that is regulated and safe. I am someone who personally benefited from government-issued student loans so that I could attend college. This is something that I will forever be grateful for, as there would have been no other way for me to achieve the level of education I had otherwise. Many of my friends and family members benefited firsthand from government programs and subsidies and have spent their lives giving back to their community because of it. We were also very fortunate to live in a city that, on the brink of collapse, was "saved" by the community coming together to support lowering pensions, with hard-working blue-collar folks making individual sacrifices for the greater good of the whole. Alexandria Ocasio-Cortez puts herself on the line every day for that greater good.

I truly appreciate that my celebrity has afforded me many opportunities to speak publicly and to step outside my "comfort zone" and shine a light on others who deserve to be recognized and supported. A few years ago, I was offered the honor of speaking at the Women's March in Los Angeles. I wasn't sure what to say, or how to say it. Fortunately, my wife, Elle (a bright, fearless soul and, like AOC, a fighter for all that is just in the world), was there to inspire me. I started by sharing with the crowd what I had learned firsthand by watching her—a female producer and director who works ten times as hard as many of the men around her and rarely gets even half the credit. And she's not alone. There are plenty of women who stand up for what they know is right every single day; even if it means they will get ridiculed for it. There are qualified women who get passed over for promotions, women who are called names for showing strength, and women who work tirelessly behind the scenes to help change and shape the world and we don't even know who they are. So when someone like AOC comes along and isn't afraid to set an example, to stand up for what is right and just and knock some holes in that glass ceiling, it is a perfect time for me to use my voice and help shine that light.

My personal hope is that one day you'll pick up this compendium to give it a nostalgic perusal, show it to your grandchildren, point out a conspicuous autograph on one of the pages, and say, "She signed this for me before she became president."

AOC

INTRODUCTION: The Meaning of AOC

Lynda Lopez

Under the elevated subway train on Westchester Avenue in the Bronx, the part that runs between Castle Hill Avenue and Parkchester, is a vibrant, multicultural, bustling stretch of main drag that somehow manages all at once to feel big city and exactly like home. The road goes past the El Texano restaurant, the Beauty Bar, and the Dollar Tree; it runs up to the main entrance of the Parkchester stop of the 6 train, where a handful of riders exit the station's doors and pour out into the street every few minutes all day long. Though the subway's relentless rumbling and the earsplitting screeches of its brakes can be heard, and felt, throughout the day, there is none of the frenetic energy here that you'd find in Manhattan. It's a low-key and almost quiet outer-borough neighborhood, of mostly black and Latino residents. And in the space right next to the Parkchester branch of the New York Public Library (across from the McDonald's and the Catholic Guardian Services building) is the Bronx district office of the youngest woman ever elected to Congress. It is in the neighborhood where she was born, and now lives. And it sits just blocks from where I grew up, in the Castle Hill section of the Bronx.

From the beginning, there was something that intrigued me about Alexandria Ocasio-Cortez—her stunning win over a ten-term incumbent New York congressman and the policy positions that were blowing people's minds with a progressivism we hadn't seen from a political newcomer in a while, to be sure. But it was looking at her Westchester Avenue district office address, and seeing her apply red lipstick in the small bathroom of her Bronx apartment in the documentary *Knock Down the House*, that drew me in a different way. There was some innate understanding there; something that made me want to root for her. It felt not just familiar, it felt as if it validated my being. It made me think of all the women I knew who came before, who put on lipstick in those same small bathroom mirrors. The ones who went out into the world without privilege or a leg up, and raised all of us daughters to go out in that world, steeled by their strength and lessons in self-reliance; the ones who taught us to survive so that the next generation could thrive. Ocasio-Cortez made it clear she came to this run for Congress to make her district, our neighborhood, a better, easier, more successful (more fruitful) place to live.

And when you come from this place, it's hard not to root for that.

I loved my mostly Puerto Rican neighborhood growing up, and still do, but even then, it was hard to ignore its challenges—the simple realities of the struggles here that still exist today. The local child poverty rate is a staggering 40 percent. In health outcomes for its residents, the Bronx ranks dead last in the state of New York: 62nd out of 62 counties, when counting health factors such as obesity rates, smoking, mental health, the quality of air and water, access to healthy foods, unemployment, and income inequality. Schools here are at 105 percent capacity.[1] The poorest of the country's 435 congressional districts is in the Bronx. The economic realities of this place mean that, for most residents, the security of enough doesn't exist; lack defines the lives of too many.

Whenever I find myself back in this neighborhood, my mind is never far from the grit, strength, and hustle it takes to press through the everyday stress and try to live your best possible life here. If you grow up or raise a family in this neighborhood, your permanent dream is of doing better, even as you know not many around you will rise. Being from here—a good friend I grew up with in the Bronx explained to me once—means that "We have to dream big. We have no choice."

It's from this place that I got on the 6 train for the first time, on my own, to go into Manhattan for my first job when I was a high school senior. A true musical theater nerd, I answered an ad one day looking for young part-timers to sell programs and souvenirs in the lobbies of Broadway theaters. My dream gig! Even if it involved riding the subway four days a week to make $15 a shift working for two hours a night. And because I looked as I did, and was from the place I was from, on one of my first days of work as I folded T-shirts at a souvenir booth, one of the ushers at the theater asked me, "You're Puerto Rican? And you're seventeen? Where's your three kids?" And then laughed uproariously with his white friends.

I remember that experience so clearly because it was that "first" most kids of color have when we are young—the first time encountering someone who believes that the fact that we are Latina means they can mock us, that they think we are somehow less than them. It was the very first time I had the thought—I didn't voice it, though I should have—"Who, exactly, do you think I am? Who am I supposed to be, according to you?"

Ocasio-Cortez was born in the Bronx in 1989. Four years before she was born a study called the Puerto Rican community in New York "a people in poverty and a community in crisis." It concluded that Puerto Ricans were one of the poorest ethnic groups in the country, "if not the poorest." The community's low economic and social status despite being American citizens, the report argued, was due to a variety of factors, including discrimination and, sometimes, a language barrier.[2]

Ocasio-Cortez was living in this reality in the Bronx when her parents decided to move the family to a suburb 40 minutes north. It was meant to be a step toward a better outcome for her life, but it didn't suddenly set the family in economic stability. The loss of her father while she was in college meant that, after graduating, she worked to help her mother fight off foreclosure of their home. Her mother still eventually had to sell the house, and Alexandria moved back to the Bronx. It's from that place that she decided to run for Congress.

And as soon as she was victorious in her primary race against Democratic incumbent Joe Crowley, she immediately (in our modern media age), found herself the target of relentless policy and personal attacks. When it seemed she was being disingenuous about where she actually lived during her early school years, opponents pounced. One tweet in particular showed a photo of the family's modest house in suburban Yorktown Heights. The author of the tweet called it "a far cry from the Bronx hood upbringing she's selling." Though it was clear he mostly just wanted to call her out, I couldn't brush past "the Bronx hood" remark. "Bronx hood upbringing." What, exactly, does that mean to you? Who is she supposed to be, according to you?

So as someone who intimately knows where she is from, and as a reporter and journalist, I recognized that her significance went beyond her as Personality or Famous Politician. Her win, coupled with her wildly impressive social media savvy, was enabling her to force the media to cover and politicians to address some of the most pressing—and most pushed aside—issues of our time, including poverty, gender and racial economic disparities, massive and unsustainable income inequality, and the urgency around environmental issues. And the communities most affected by those issues responded to her. But particularly, for Latina women who watched her get sworn into Congress standing next to her mother and brother, with her hoop earrings, red lipstick, and dark hair swept back, there was a swell of power, positivity, and pride.

But AOC is not just culturally symbolic. She is a symbol meeting a moment, a particular American moment that is massively important to communities not used to having their voices heard. Her unabashed willingness to take up space, stand in her power, and speak loudly for the underserved and underprivileged, makes her a standout to those communities—and also in Washington. Maria Teresa Kumar, founder of Voto Latino, notes that AOC is one of the most effective communicators in D.C. "I don't think she's just changed the conversation in the country, she's helping define it. No one in the country doesn't know what the Green New Deal is. That is not small. And for her to do that out of the gate, less than three months into her congressional seat, again, not small." AOC's ability to communicate her aspirational legislation, and move people to join her, like Senator Ed Markey of Massachusetts, who agreed to sponsor the Green New Deal with her, is one of the factors that make her so significant in national politics now. And Kumar says that it's not just her biggest or most far-reaching policies and proposals that made her a force from the beginning; it's the smaller ones, as well.

AOC's insistence on a living wage for her congressional staff, Kumar believes, was transformational. "I used to be a congressional staffer. When I got to Congress, I was earning so little . . . that I was considering taking on another job. That sounds fine, except when you're a legislative aid, you might work until 3 or 4 o'clock in the morning. I was getting paid so little that I qualified for low-income housing. A starting salary of $54,000 a year (for AOC's staff) is not only a living wage, it allows someone of my background, who did not have connections, to be at the table. It allows for you not to be shut out of the market because you actually couldn't do it, financially. *That* is not small.

"A lot of the young people who are on Capitol Hill are subsidized by their parents. That was never an option for me. AOC, all of a sudden, created a real meritocracy by allowing anyone to apply, regardless of zip code."

Simply observing some of these aspirational and far-reaching policy goals of AOC's would be worthy of an entire book. The fact that she is a Puerto Rican woman representing her district in Congress is also noteworthy—even after the 2018 midterm elections ushered in record numbers of women and people of color, the number of women in Congress only rose by 3 percent. But most significantly, AOC matters because she rose at this moment in our country's story and discourse.

Latinos in the United States have always known discrimination. They have always experienced prejudice. But particularly in the administration during which Ocasio-Cortez was sworn in, it is not an overstatement to say that Latinos feel under a new kind of attack—one that starts from the top, from a president who refused to decry white nationalists, who spews at best xenophobic and at worst racist diatribes against entire communities of color. From anti-Latino rhetoric targeted at immigrants, to a policy of child separations at the southern border, to being targeted in mass shootings at a Walmart, the climate that has been created for Latinos is one of fear, of being seen as Other. That climate makes it all the more significant that a young working-class Puerto Rican woman from the Bronx has become the most visible and effective new voice in politics. To dismiss or diminish her (as critics, including the president, do) is to ignore something larger and more meaningful that she represents.

It seems fitting, then, to explore the significance of Alexandria Ocasio-Cortez now, to look not only at her politics and context but also at her deeper impact. The essays in *AOC* check in with people from the communities to whom she has meant the most, and truly range from the personal to the political. Rebecca Traister notes that in Congress, AOC is exerting the same power as a man— and a woman who governs like a man is a perceived threat, around whom all manner of negative narrative can spring. Keegan-Michael Key celebrates AOC's passion and fighting spirit. Nathan Robinson discusses why a label of "democratic socialism" has a slightly different meaning to young people and millennials like Ocasio-Cortez, while Patricia Reynoso writes about feeling as if other Latinas who succeeded didn't come from the same place she did—until AOC appeared. Erin Aubry Kaplan notes that it took courage for AOC to dance unapologetically outside her congressional office after some tried to ridicule her for a college dancing video that had gone viral, and that same courage is required when talking about race and color in politics. Pedro Regalado writes about the long and rich history of Puerto Rican activism in AOC's native New York City, while Wendy Carrillo tells of how witnessing the Dakota Access Pipeline protest at Standing Rock was critical to her and to AOC running for office. Natalia Sylvester speaks of how she realized that the imperfect bilingualism she shares with AOC is a beautiful superpower—after a lifetime of being embarrassed by it. Carmen Rita Wong writes about the boldness and braveness it takes, as a Latina, to speak truth to power in the financial realm, and Tracey Ross discusses how AOC highlights the conversation about poverty—and the people it affects. Longtime environmental activist Elizabeth Yeampierre writes about AOC's willingness to listen to criticism and how that makes her a unique politician. Journalist Mariana Atencio observes the power of AOC's social media savvy and how she puts it to use. Prisca Dorcas Mojica Rodriguez talks about how hard it can be to be indignant, like herself and this new millennial congresswoman. María Christina (MC) González Noguera shares her own story to illustrate the importance of the ties between Puerto Rico and its citizens here in the U.S., as represented by leaders like AOC. Jennine Capó Crucet simply penned an open letter to the congresswoman, an appreciation. And Andrea González-Ramírez gives the primer, the origin story of AOC, from her early life to her historic congressional win, and beyond.

I recently remembered that the night Ocasio-Cortez won her primary, my father had texted me and my two sisters together. He typed just two words: "Alexandria won!" I had no idea before this that my dad, who now lives on the West Coast, even followed what was happening politically in our old neighborhood, nor had he mentioned that he was aware of the race. And though he said nothing else, we all three knew exactly what he meant—a young woman, who was from the same place where he raised his three daughters, had defeated the powerful machine that protected the kind of leadership he had always known there. It meant that we are were moving in a direction my

dad had dreamed of for nearly all of his almost 80 years—
toward a better place than where our country has been recently. And though he knew as well as we did that AOC's
story had only just begun, and there would be many steps,
good and bad, for her along the way, he wanted us to know
how happy he was that we had all (including Alexandria)
dreamed big. He knew we had had no choice.

An Open Letter to Congresswoman Ocasio-Cortez

Jennine Capó Crucet

Just writing those words—*Congresswoman Ocasio-Cortez*—
makes me want to jump in place, still stings my eyes, even
all these months later. How to explain what you mean to
us—to me—without sounding like a freak or a fangirl
(though yeah, I am probably both, and you'd probably tell
me to just own it, no shame)? How to get it across without
putting even more weight than you no doubt already have
on your shoulders? It's likely impossible, but so was your
win, according to so many "experts" you proved wrong.
And it's with that hope and in that spirit that I write this.

I watched your brilliant, ambitious campaign from half-
way across the country (I'm from Miami but I live in Nebraska right now—long story) with much hope and with a
kind of dread, thinking I already knew the ending; like you,
I'd often been exactly the right person for an opportunity,

and many times I'd been kept from it because of forces outside my control—my Latinidad, my working-class roots, my gender, my youth. And when I watched in real time your reaction to the announcement that you'd won the Democratic primary in your district—your hand over your mouth, your eyes wide open with surprise—I realized that you'd held that same seed of dread all along: that you, too, were shocked to see you'd done it, that while you'd of course hoped for that result, you'd also been through enough and seen enough to know that protecting yourself against a possible loss by holding on to that seed wasn't foolish—it is how we survive each day in this America.

That feeling of astonishment that comes when our hope and brilliance really and truly pay off (against all odds and the expectations of those who purport to know better): I've experienced that feeling. And the night you stared at the screen, in a shock stemming from the true extent of the revolution you'd started, I saw in your face my own face. I remembered an afternoon ten years ago, when my phone rang and a number I didn't recognize flashed on its screen. I almost didn't pick up. I almost didn't get to hear the news that I'd become the first Latinx woman ever to win the Iowa Short Fiction Award—an award given to a debut book of short stories, an award that, for the 39 years prior to me winning it, had only been won by white writers. Four decades in, and a Latina—me—had finally broken into the literary house with a book about working-class Latinos from the city of Hialeah—a neighborhood I rep with the same pride you rep the Bronx. I was 26 years old, the oldest daughter from a family of electricians. The prize officially started my writing career in a way that the established literary community would recognize. I almost didn't apply, thinking the odds were skewed too far against someone like me. When I recently watched the documentary *Knock Down the House* on Netflix, I had to pause the movie after that part where you tell your niece that the way to win everything is to get rejected maybe ten times first—that's how it works in publishing, too. It's probably how things work for everything we try to do, and you delivered that advice with a huge smile that I couldn't help but mirror in the darkness of my living room. We shared that smile even in the face of the ugly truth that your advice works to combat.

Whenever I watch you on TV doing your job in Congress, I want to step through the screen and stand next to you with my arms crossed, my hip cocked, daring anyone who might mess with you to fight me. (I've been working out and am surprisingly strong for my size and also extremely scrappy.) I believe there's safety in numbers, and based on who you choose to sit next to in the House, I know you know this, too. I think I get so instinctually protective of you, sitting there asking the smartest questions, because (a) that's how I was raised and (b) I know that feeling too: I was almost always the only Latina in my classes in college (was it like that for you at Boston University?); I was the only Latina in my whole graduate creative writing program all three years I was there; I was the only Latina in my department at my first professor job, which came a couple years after my first book came out. I often felt lonely and angry and scared and wished for an ally. It's no wonder I want to project myself through time and space, muscle myself through all the security, plant myself behind your desk, make myself a real-life version of *Key & Peele*'s Obama anger translator, Luther. I would spew all the cusses and throw all the punches you can't. But not like Luther, not for laughs: I'd be there the way our women have always been there for each other—to keep ourselves safe and sane and seen.

While in graduate school, where I studied fiction writing, a white woman in my program wrote a critique of one of my short stories in which she "joked" that I should change all my characters from Cuban to Mexican "just for fun." She went on to say that she didn't know how to help me, because all my writing was clearly doing "the Latina thing." With that phrase, this woman was trying to eliminate everything I'd done, everything I'd worked for, everyone and everything I cared about. She didn't see my characters as people worth her attention. She was sure I'd figure out what to do on my own.

Years later, when that psycho from Fox News (whom I will not even name because she does not deserve a name here) tried to minimize you using the exact same phrase, you did something I didn't have the guts to do back then: you defined for yourself what "the Latina thing" meant, turned it into a rallying cry. You took to Twitter and said, "If by 'the Latina thing,' she means I actually do the work instead of just talk about it, then yeah, I'm doing 'the Latina thing.'"

I still have that white woman's critique. It lives in a box with more of the same kind of evidence, a box that has followed me through several cross-country moves. I saved it and everything else for all the same reasons that you took that same phrase and turned it into a call to action, something I'm tempted to put on a T-shirt and wear while on my next book tour.

Damn right we're doing the Latina thing.

I hadn't thought of that phrase—"the Latina thing"—in a long time, not until Fox News tried to hurt you with it. But by your definition, I've been living it. In the years since that writer tried to tear down my work with those three little words, I had been hard at work on a novel, which I wrote for a college version of me who needed to see her experiences as a first-generation American and a first-generation college student represented on the page. And I wrote it for the three Latinx students I met while I worked for an LA-based nonprofit, students who asked me for a story that could help guide them as they moved through predominantly white spaces after having been raised in communities where almost everyone looked and spoke like them. I wrote it for you, too, though I didn't know it yet. And I'd also become a professor: it wasn't a job I was supposed to land, but I proved to enough people that I was the best person for the position and left my nonprofit counseling job behind. Just as your work in hospitality has proven vital to your tenure as a congressperson, my counseling work has prepared me for many elements of my professor job. Basically, like you said, I've been actually doing the work instead of just talking about it.

This past spring, at a conference, I ran into that white woman from grad school, the one who'd used the phrase "the Latina thing" to describe my work. This woman had published a couple books herself; it is not arrogant—only accurate—for me to say that I've had more success in my writing career than she has. She identifies as a progressive, a liberal, and she now calls New York home (she's not your constituent, though she wishes she were). Seeing her at the conference, I had been ready to walk past her and pretend we didn't know each other, to protect myself against the old hurt that seeing her had immediately brought up in me. (Can you even do this in your job? No, right? What do you say now to those people, your colleagues, who never imagined you there?) She got in my way, stopped me on my route to somewhere else. And just as my gut had predicted, she managed to offend me in all the same old ways: she said she was stunned at how well my writing career was going. "You're just everywhere!" she said. "It's crazy!" This woman said this in a way that communicated she thought I was dumb enough to not see her "compliment" for what it really was—a dig, a dis. She was still underestimating me. She kept saying how "crazy" it was that I now write for the *New York Times*, that I had a new book already coming out—that of all of us from that MFA program, I seemed to be thriving against all odds.

She's not wrong about the odds: My publisher gave my last novel—about a young Latinx woman, the first in her family to go away to college—very little support, which is not atypical for first books, especially those by women of color. But it found a hungry audience anyway because the book was desperately needed by a sizable group of people whom the (largely white) publishing industry both repeatedly ignores and repeatedly underestimates. In many ways, the whole experience of that novel coming into the world was a microcosm of your district, of our government, of our potential for substantial and needed change.

I played nice with this woman but I did not give in to her easy agreement that yeah, it's just nuts that my novel is doing so well. Nor did I cuss at or punch her, but that's because time has mellowed me with regard to this particular offense. What I did do was think of you. I thought of how you smiled at your niece in the documentary, how you reframed the intended insult from Fox News (which these days mentions you nonstop—that's how much you scare them, that's how powerful a symbol you've become). And in thinking of you in this moment—a new reflex, a muscle newly tensed and utilized—I came to understand your power not just as a symbol, but as a living, recognizable being—a sister I wished I could call or text later to talk about this moment, how it all went down. And I had never in my life had so strong a response to a politician—which made me realize that my whole life, though I'd sometimes seen my political beliefs reflected in the choices elected officials supposedly made on my behalf, before you, I'd never felt truly represented by anyone in our government. And this realization made me both angry and determined to keep fighting.

So yeah, I thought of you and interrupted this ghost woman as she continued to express how bizarre she found it that I'd somehow managed to become a successful writer. I said, "I know—but it's not so much crazy as it's about freaking time. And yeah, I'm killing it. I'm totally killing it."

The woman had nothing to say—maybe she was offended by the confidence she'd long thought she'd undermined—but eventually stuttered, "Yeah, totally," before I said I had a meeting to get to, that it was lovely seeing her again.

The invitation to write this essay came on the heels of that interaction. And because I was raised to believe in signs, I think it was meant to be that I tell you this now: AOC, you are totally killing it. YOU ARE TOTALLY KILLING IT. You are doing the Latina thing and staying true to yourself; you won the primary by being yourself, not by "toning it down"—the message I got again and again. I was conditioned away from being myself, having been the only one of me in a room so many times before. My training in predominantly white spaces told me to mute who I was, not embrace it: I was told by white gatekeepers to *tone it down*, to stop talking with my hands, to hold back what they called my sass. *Be less fierce, less emotional, less angry.* This conditioning was so strong that I even caught myself reflexively channeling this advice to *you* when I watched you debate Joe Crowley. In that televised debate, you had your face set, and I could read the tension in your jaw and know that you were clearly angry, or clearly shocked, or clearly amused. You couldn't hide it. You didn't even try to hide it. You reminded me of myself before the machine of grad school had ground me down to almost nothing. When you talked, your hands did, too. You banged on the table like a kind of punctuation—the same way my mother and sister do, the same way I do—disturbing the microphones. I found myself cringing, pulling back on your behalf, thinking, *Be careful! I love this and I love seeing a normal person talking the way I always have, but please God, keep it under control! We are on their turf!* But I also instantly recognized this response as my conditioning from grad school, where these things were trained out of me, where I was reprogrammed in a way that actually *took away* my power while purporting to give me access to power—power that, through my voice, I'd already had. Watching that debate, watching you in Congress now, you are teaching me a new way to be—which is just this: the way I already am, who I've always been. This is our turf, too.

The only place I never stopped being my true self was

on the page, writing characters who looked and sounded like the real me—like you—because that was my only goal: to tell stories about the lives of people I knew and loved, to do my best to represent them in such a way that it gave them a place in literature. It's ambitious and some days it feels impossible, until I realize I'm already doing it with every word I write. I think of you in your office doing the Latina thing, and I get back to work.

In the Netflix documentary, one of the longtime organizers helping you in your campaign tells you, "Nobody owns you yet." It's the *yet* that scares me. It's the *yet* that compels me to write this. When I see you at work, I see a version of myself, of the women I went to high school with, the women in my family. And it makes me realize how I haven't really seen women like that in charge of our government, and how we've all suffered for it. I see how Fox News is trying to tear you down. They understand how charismatic and magnetic you are, and they are trying to kill that in you. On a smaller scale, that's been the story of my publishing career, of my academic career, and I just see you at the start of it and want to throw away the playbook I was handed—*keep your voice down, stop talking with your hands*—and be my real self again. We are hungry to see ourselves really and truly represented, and there is nothing you have to do to be that for us except not fall into that *yet*.

My fear is that knowing how much you mean to us will put too much pressure on you. I still feel this pressure myself when I visit colleges where girls like me have read my book and ask me such hard questions: *When do these bad feelings go away? How do we stand up in the face of so much corruption and adversity?* The answer is always us; in loving and valuing each other and ourselves, we gain the strength and momentum each day anew to keep fighting. All our heroines—you among them—are teaching us this lesson, one page in history at a time. And so I've learned that this pressure we feel is not pressure at all; it's the force of our ancestors buoying us brightly forward. It's their invisible hands cupping our shoulder blades, their flat palms pushing against our spines, a literal sensation to remind us that we have each other's backs.

I'm writing in the end to ask: Do you want to be friends? Because we already are. My new book is a collection of essays called *My Time Among the Whites,* and it's basically about your new job, more or less. Let me know and I'll send you a copy; you don't know it, but you helped me write it, and at the same time, I wrote it for you—for the *us* we've always been part of. Like everything I write, it's my way of showing you what you meant to me, to us. It's my way of saying thank you.

Women Like Me Aren't Supposed to Run for Office

Andrea González-Ramírez

Alexandria Ocasio-Cortez was not supposed to win New York's 14th congressional district. Not based on history, or statistics, or even common sense. And yet, on June 26, 2018, Ocasio-Cortez defeated Rep. Joseph "Joe" Crowley—then the fourth-highest-ranking Democrat in the U.S. House of Representatives—in the primary, instantly jump-starting her political career. In her unlikely path to office, she was unwavering in championing and defending what she believed was morally right.

"We have had our country on autopilot, and we've been accepting what's been happening," she told me in an interview for Refinery29 two weeks before that fateful election night.[1] "And what's happening in this country is indicative that we need new leadership. We need new leadership in the Democratic Party and we need new leadership in the country." By "what's happening in this country" she meant the systematic problems burdening her constituency and most Americans: income inequality, rising health care costs, crushing student debt, the accelerating threat of climate change, an epidemic of gun violence, the affordable housing crisis, and, of course, the forces that allowed the rise of President Donald Trump.

Ocasio-Cortez is, without a doubt, a new kind of leader. Against all odds, she defeated Crowley with 57 percent of the vote. Her primary win guaranteed she would be elected by her district, which is as blue as they come, in the midterm election and would make history as the youngest woman ever elected to Congress.[2] But long before she became the "Wonder Woman of the left, Wicked Witch of the right," she was just a young woman trying to survive in America.[3]

Alexandria Ocasio-Cortez was born in New York City on October 13, 1989, the eldest child of Sergio Ocasio-Roman, an architect from the South Bronx, and Blanca Ocasio-Cortez (née Cortez), a domestic worker from Puerto Rico. "Her dad and I were preparing for Alexandria's birth and still picking names," Blanca told the *Daily Mail Online*.[4] "And he came up with 'Alexandria.' I thought about it for a while and I said: 'Alexandria Ocasio-Cortez. That sounds very powerful.'"

Alexandria and her younger brother, Gabriel, spent the early years of their lives in the Parkchester neighborhood of the Bronx, a working-class and diverse community. But when she was around five years old, the Ocasio-Cortezes packed their bags and moved 40 minutes north to the Westchester County suburb of Yorktown Heights; their extended family had helped them scrape enough money together for a down payment on a modest two-bedroom house.[5] The hope was that Alexandria and Gabriel would have a shot at a better education in Yorktown Heights—a more affluent neighborhood with better schools—and, therefore, a shot at a better life.

"I was born in a place where my zip code determined my destiny. And my parents did everything in their power to move me out of that zip code," Ocasio-Cortez told *Latino USA* of the family's decision to leave the Bronx, a borough in which 52 percent of the neighborhoods are below the poverty line.[6]

Around the time of her family's move, the rate at which Latino students in New York City dropped out of high school was over 25 percent.[7] "I grew up feeling like that was an injustice. The fact that I had to move away from my family, in order to get the same chance that any other American kid should get."

"Sandy," as her family and friends affectionately call her, says she was a "dorky kid."[8] She was a driven student, the type who asked her parents for a microscope on her birthday, who read the *New York Times* daily, and who at one point in her childhood wanted to become an obstetrician or gynecologist.[9] In 2007, she won second place in the microbiology category at the Intel International Science and Engineering Fair for her project on the effects of antioxidants on the life span of roundworms.[10] As a prize, an asteroid was named after her: the 23238 Ocasio-Cortez.[11]

Her high school science teacher, Michael Blueglass, told the *New York Times* that Alexandria's passion for science often had a political lens.[12] "She was interested in research to help people in all areas, including developing nations, not just for the people with money," he said. That nascent political consciousness was developed in great part because of her father, Sergio. "I would always ask about the world. Even when I was a kid, he always treated me like an adult in these conversations," she said.[13] "He didn't hide the ugliness of the world for me.

"He would just say, 'This is what it is.' And I would say, 'Well, we need to fix that.' And he was like, 'Yes, we do.' "

Alexandria grew up aware that she was different from most of her neighbors in the Yorktown Heights community. "I went to public school in a town where no one looked like me," she said in the documentary *Knock Down the House*.[14] Yorktown Heights is nearly 90 percent white and the median household income is around $115,000.[15] Even though Alexandria and her family had made it out of the Bronx, they were by no means well-off. "In any affluent area there's an underclass of people who serve the people who live there," she said.[16] "And that's what my family was. My mom cleaned the houses of the kinds of people who I went to school with. And my dad really struggled to start his own small business . . . It was really picking up towards actually the end of his life." Oftentimes Blanca would clean houses in exchange for her clients tutoring her daughter for the SAT. Ocasio-Cortez said that their family friends in the area were typically other workers like her parents, to whom they could relate.

When Alexandria was 16, Sergio was diagnosed with a rare form of lung cancer. By then his architecture business was going well, but he had no health insurance.[17] Cancer's financial fallout disrupts the lives of millions of Americans: around 42 percent of patients drain their life savings within two years of their diagnosis.[18] The Ocasio-Cortez family was not immune to the financial strain. "He was in experimental trials in order to save his life," Ocasio-Cortez said of her father's illness at a prescription drug prices hearing held by the House Committee on Oversight and Reform in July 2019.[19] "My family almost lost our home in order to try to keep him alive and just try to keep our family together."

Despite the financial difficulties the family faced, their sacrifices paid off. When she graduated high school, Alexandria pooled enough money together from student loans and scholarships to attend Boston University.[20] She chose the science track, majoring in biochemistry.

But as she was starting her sophomore year in the fall of 2008, she got a call from home: Her father was dying. They had a very close relationship.[21] "My father knew my soul better than anyone else on this planet," she said in *Knock Down the House*. "He really made me believe I had true power in this world."

Sergio Ocasio-Roman died on September 8, 2008. He was 48.

His passing was a destabilizing force for every member of the family. "My mother was done. My brother was lost. I took it hard, too, but I channeled it into my studies. That's how I dealt with it. I was home for a week and went right back to school," Alexandria told the *New Yorker*.[22] "The last thing my father had told me in the hospital was 'Make me proud.' I took it very literally. My G.P.A. skyrocketed."

Alexandria decided to shift her focus from science, changing her major to economics and international relations. She began to really thrive at BU, making the dean's list.[23] She worked part-time in the Boston office of the late senator Edward "Ted" Kennedy, a Democrat, where she focused on foreign affairs and immigration services. At BU, Alexandria led "Coffee and Conversations," Friday-afternoon student discussions, where she debated everything from public policy to the meaning of love. (It was in one of those meetings that she met her partner, Riley Roberts, a fellow student and now a web developer.[24] They broke up in college but reconnected in their midtwenties.) She launched the student group Alianza Latina and spent a semester abroad in Niger during her junior year before graduating cum laude in 2011.[25]

Ocasio-Cortez's father died at the height of the 2008 financial crisis, and it was nearly impossible for the family to recover financially. To make ends meet, her mother, Blanca, had become a school bus driver in addition to cleaning houses. At one point, Blanca also worked as a hospital receptionist. "After my husband died, the family went through tough times," Blanca said.[26] "Alexandria was in college, but I still had her little brother who needed to be put through school." The family was trying to prevent their house from being foreclosed on while fighting a probate battle with the Westchester County Surrogate's Court because Sergio had died without a will.[27] Despite Alexandria's growth as a student and a leader, after she graduated, she was forced to return to her family's Bronx apartment, which they owned in addition to their Yorktown Heights home, and begin working as a waitress to pitch in.

Like many other young people who came of age after the recession, Alexandria spent most of her early postgrad years living paycheck to paycheck. In 2012, at 22, she launched Brook Avenue Press, a children's literature publisher that sought to portray the Bronx in a positive way.[28] She was also an educator at the National Hispanic Institute. And at night, she would mix drinks and wait tables to supplement her income. By the time she ran for office, she was working at a taqueria called Flats Fix in Manhattan's Union Square. She told *Time* magazine that her health insurance plan, which she obtained through the Affordable Care Act, cost about $200 a month and had a massive deductible.[29] She had about $25,000 in student loan debt from her undergraduate education, which translated to a monthly payment of about $300.

Her time in the service industry led Alexandria to internalize the message that your value as a person is tied to your income. She has talked about being sexually harassed and how she felt inferior because of the way patrons often treated her.[30] Her experiences contributed to her political awakening when Senator Bernie Sanders entered the 2016 presidential election, challenging Hillary Clinton from the left in the Democratic primary. "It wasn't until I heard of a man by the name of Bernie Sanders that I began to question and assert and recognize my inherent value as a human being that deserves health care, housing, education and a living wage," she said at a campaign rally with Sanders in October 2019.[31]

Sanders's message of empowerment and equality hit all the right notes with Alexandria, and soon she was working as an organizer on his campaign. Around the same time in 2016, Blanca sold their family home in Yorktown Heights. They had twice fended off a foreclosure, but Blanca struggled to keep up with the rising cost of living in New York. With her two kids out of college, she moved to Florida.

Alexandria attributes her knack for organizing to her parents. She has said they were not outwardly political but naturally gravitated toward creating a sense of community.[32] "They were always about leaning in to people. And the politics comes second," she said. "That's how I practice, as well. Even though I feel very strongly about my beliefs, my number one job is to care about people and to lean in."

Sanders later lost the Democratic primary, and Donald Trump became president. In December 2016, Alexandria and a few friends crammed into a borrowed 1998 Subaru and drove all the way to Standing Rock Indian Reservation in North Dakota.[33] At the time, the Lakota Sioux had been protesting for months against the Dakota Access Pipeline, arguing it would pollute the reservation's water supplies and endanger the tribe's sacred sites. Along the way, Alexandria's group stopped in Flint, Michigan, which had been struggling with a crisis of lead-poisoned water for years after the city changed its water supply to save money.[34]

The trip was transformational for Alexandria. "It was really from that crucible of activism where I saw people putting their lives on the line . . . for people they've never met and never known," she said in late 2018.[35] "When I saw that, I knew that I had to do something more."

As she was on her way back to New York, her phone rang.

In 2016, a group of Sanders campaign alums created Brand New Congress (BNC) with the purpose of recruiting progressive candidates who were not prototypically white, wealthy, and politically connected. Alexandria's brother, Gabriel, a real estate agent at the time, nominated her after the group solicited suggestions of community leaders who might be up to the task. She fit their mold perfectly—and they reached out.

Alexandria had never really thought of becoming a politician. "I never liked the culture of what it meant to run for office. I love serving people. And that's always kind of been my mission and my drive," she told me in June 2018. "I never really saw this for myself. Especially in New York City, the political culture is so aggressive. It's so driven by big money. And it's so driven by dynastic power. I just felt like it wasn't who I was."

In the spring of 2017, Alexandria attended a BNC candidate recruitment meeting in Knoxville, Tennessee. By the summer, she was already campaigning in New York's 14th congressional district, knocking on doors and spending time in people's living rooms, pitching her candidacy. She emphasized she was not challenging Crowley from the left. Instead, she framed the race as a top-vs.-bottom one. She identifies as a democratic socialist, just like Sanders, and her platform reflected that.[36] She advocated for Medicare for All, a $15-per-hour minimum wage, abolishing U.S. Immigration and Customs Enforcement (ICE), and a federal jobs guarantee.

"While it's not that nothing has happened in the Bronx, it feels that we are dealing with the same problems 20 years later," she told me at the time. "I'm an organizer here and I know no one ever sees [Crowley]; he doesn't have a presence in this community. It would be different if he was around." She added: "This is why I'm challenging this seat. It's because we deserve real representation and not representation that phoned it in. Our community deserves better, especially our community which is 70 percent people of color, half Latino, overwhelmingly immigrant, very working class, and we can't afford representation that just doesn't even think that we're worthy of living next to." (The congressman infamously lived in Virginia, though he kept a house in Queens.[37])

Crowley was Goliath to Alexandria's David. Nicknamed the "King of Queens," he was first elected in 1999 and had not faced a primary challenger in 14 years. He was the president of the Queens County Democratic Party and was House Speaker Nancy Pelosi's presumptive heir. In the 2018 primary race, he received endorsements from every big-name Democrat in New York—from Governor Andrew Cuomo to Senators Chuck Schumer and Kirsten Gillibrand. And he had deep pockets: Alexandria only had about $250,000 to his $1.5 million war chest, according to OpenSecrets, which tracks federal campaign contributions.[38] But Alexandria persisted. She split her time between the Manhattan bar where she worked and campaign events, wearing literal holes in her shoes walking around the eastern part of the Bronx and north-central Queens.[39] Her unconventional team was made up of progressives whose only political experience was working with Bernie Sanders in 2016.[40] They included her campaign manager, Virginia Ramos Rios, and communications director, Corbin Trent, and young volunteers from eclectic backgrounds such as food blogger Naureen Akhter and heavy metal singer Jesse Korman. And it worked. Against all odds, she got on the ballot in April 2018.[41] Groups like Democratic Socialists of America (DSA) and Black Lives Matter supported her bid. Despite being outspent, the scrappy campaign went above and beyond to reach people: they made 170,000 calls, sent 120,000 text messages, and knocked on 120,000 doors in the district.[42]

Regardless, most observers believed that Alexandria—a young, working-class, Puerto Rican woman from the

Bronx—did not represent a real threat to Crowley and the Democratic establishment. A large part of the political class and the press anticipated the ten-term congressman's victory.[43]

"Women like me aren't supposed to run for office. I wasn't born into a wealthy or powerful family," she says in a viral campaign ad from May 2018.[44] Alexandria was not wrong when she said that women like her have historically been denied access to the halls of power. Before the 2018 mid-term election—which brought an unprecedented number of women and people of color to Washington—the 115th Congress was among the oldest of any in recent history.[45] The average age for lawmakers was 58 in the House and 62 in the Senate, while the U.S. median age is 37 years old.[46] And there was barely any racial or ethnic diversity on Capitol Hill. At the time, the body was roughly 78 percent white and 80 percent male.[47] By contrast, women make up more than half of the U.S. population and people of color nearly 40 percent.[48] Working-class Americans also did not see themselves represented: The median net worth for House members was $900,000, and for senators it was $3.2 million as of 2015.[49] The net wealth for the average American household, on the other hand, was roughly $80,000.

Crowley, understanding the party machine, came across as someone who knew he had the election in the bag. He skipped a community debate in Queens because of "scheduling conflicts," so Alexandria ended up debating an empty chair.[50] In one of the most controversial moments in the race, Crowley sent former New York City councilwoman Annabel Palma—a Latina—to face Alexandria in his place at a Bronx event while he attended a community meeting in Queens.[51] Some saw that decision as racist, with Alexandria chiming in that it was "a bizarre twist" that Crowley "sent a woman with slight resemblance to me" as a surrogate.[52] It was a big miscalculation that earned Crowley a scathing editorial in the *New York Times*, which nevertheless endorsed him.[53]

On the evening of June 26, 2018, Alexandria headed to Park Billiards and Cafe in the Bronx, where her election night party was taking place. The campaign had finally raised enough money to hold a poll, which had her losing in a landslide.[54] But when she arrived, the TV screens showed the results of the race. To her utter amazement, she had dethroned Crowley by a margin of about 4,000 votes.

The moment was captured on live TV.[55] "I cannot believe these numbers right now," she said. "But I do know that every single person here has worked their butts off to change the future of the Bronx and Queens."

Alexandria delivered the biggest political upset in recent history. But she has always made clear that the victory was bigger than her. "We meet a machine with a movement," she told her supporters, "and that's what we did today."

The AOC phenomenon had just begun.

In the months following the primary, Alexandria traveled around the country to campaign for other progressive candidates who could potentially re-create her stunning victory.[56] Only two of them, Rashida Tlaib of Michigan and Ayanna Pressley of Massachusetts, did. The decision to use her meteoric rise to support primary challengers immediately rattled the Democratic establishment.[57] She also quickly became a boogeyman for the right, with pundits pouncing to criticize her ideology and so much more, including her clothes, her childhood home, her bank account, and even her dancing.[58]

It was just a hint of how Alexandria—now dubbed AOC—would disrupt Washington. Just one week after the 2018 midterm election, Alexandria joined young climate activists in a sit-in protest urging Representative Nancy Pelosi, who was set to become the next House Speaker, to take swift action on the issue of climate change.[59] It was an unlikely move by a newly elected member of Congress to challenge the top brass like this. But Pelosi praised the young activists.[60] In early December, Alexandria criticized the fact that several events hosted by the Harvard Kennedy School for new members of Congress were full of lobbyists and CEOs.[61] That same unwavering moral compass that got her the seat was ruffling feathers in Washington. In a December interview, Senator Claire McCaskill—a veteran Democrat who had just lost her seat—called Alexandria "a bright shiny new object."[62] Others worried that she would threaten the unity of the Democratic caucus, which had a slim majority.[63] Alexandria remained unfazed, often deploying scorching comebacks at her critics and refusing to kowtow to the status quo.

At the same time, she had other concerns. As one of the few working-class members of Congress, Alexandria was trying to figure out how to get by in the transition period between the election and her first day as a lawmaker—literally. "I have three months without a salary before I'm a member of Congress. So, how do I get an apartment? Those little things are very real," she told the *New York Times*, adding that she and her partner, Riley, had saved up some money.[64] "We're kind of just dealing with the logistics of it day by day." Eventually, she found a new home in D.C.

This display of honesty, combined with her meticulous documenting of her day-to-day life as a congresswoman-elect on social media, gave her supporters an unprecedented level of access into the halls of power. Her Twitter and Instagram feeds became obsession worthy, and suddenly young women across the country began wondering whether they could run for office and win, too.[65]

On January 3, 2019, Alexandria was sworn in along with the most diverse class of freshman representatives in the history of Congress. She was dressed head-to-toe in white, with bright red lipstick and gold hoops hanging from her ears, in a classic *boricua* look that would make women in Puerto Rico and beyond very proud. In a loving Instagram post, she paid tribute to her mom, Blanca, thanking her for all the sacrifices she had made so Alexandria could succeed.[66]

There is only so much freshman members of Congress can do. But Alexandria has done the work. She introduced a resolution on the Green New Deal, the ambitious plan to tackle climate change and income inequality in the next decade.[67] She has also co-sponsored legislation on issues such as affordable housing, net neutrality, and increasing the minimum wage.[68]

Alexandria was appointed to the House Committee on Financial Services and the Committee on Oversight and Reform. Her sharp questioning during hearings on topics like dark money and big pharma often went viral.[69] In fact, her questioning of Trump's former attorney Michael Cohen effectively laid the groundwork for the Oversight Committee to subpoena the president's tax returns.[70]

She also found her squad.[71] Alexandria built a solid friendship with fellow freshman congresswomen Tlaib, Pressley, and Ilhan Omar from Minnesota as soon as they connected as congresswomen-elect. The foursome have often celebrated together and defended each other from detractors in a strong showing of sisterhood that is utterly inspiring.

Alexandria's first months in office did not go without glitches, of course. The rollout of her Green New Deal resolution was poorly executed, leading to widespread criticism.[72] It also took her team two more months than her freshman New York colleagues to open a district office.[73] Her chief of staff, Saikat Chakrabarti, resigned over the summer shortly after a public argument with a handful of moderate Democrats.[74] Being forced into the public spotlight and adapting to the aggressive learning curve of Congress took a toll on Alexandria. "The first three months or so of my term were just emotionally exhausting, like I was worried sick every single day," she told *Vogue*.[75]

And then there have been the unrelenting, racist attacks from President Trump. "Why don't they go back and help fix the totally broken and crime infested places from which they came," Trump tweeted about Alexandria and the squad, all of whom are U.S. citizens. "Then come back and show us how it is done."[76]

Despite the pressures of the job, Alexandria has remained undeterred. And yes, she's still a 30-year-old woman learning how to amass her power and use it for the greater good. But while Congress can break most people's beliefs, that doesn't seem to be the case for her. If anything, serving has solidified her belief in the politics of the possible.

"I used to be much more cynical about how much was up against us," she told *Time*. "I think I've changed my mind. Because I think that change is a lot closer than we think."[77] Before her primary win in June 2018, she told me, "We're just at a point where we need people to serve right now. We really, really need people to serve this country. And it has to be new people." Her meteoric rise proves it can even be a young, working-class, Puerto Rican woman from the Bronx.

"The First Latina to . . ."

Patricia Reynoso

Her lipstick was the first thing that I noticed. A popsicle-like red that enhanced her tan complexion without overpowering it. Its stained texture—obviously chosen for the staying power that a shiny lacquer could never deliver—took the edge off the bold hue. This lip lent congressional candidate Alexandria Ocasio-Cortez's face the kind of nonchalant glamour that I always found so hard to pull off. Paired with her Latina-girl hoops, prominent yet unpainted brows, barely made-up eyes, and sheets of glossy dark hair, the effect was more millennial Nuyorican actress than political powerhouse. This was the look of a woman aware of her good looks but who also had things to do. Like smash all kinds of records.

The swirl around the AOC campaign hit me late. Just weeks before her historic win, if I'm being honest. Once the lipstick got me, though, I quickly became one of her millions of followers on Instagram—and I don't follow politicians. Her emphatic speaking style, with the neck action and swinging arms punctuating every statement, was something I recognized intuitively. I admired her ability to clap back at haters with the swiftness of a late-night talk show host. And by the time the polls showed that this newbie from the Bronx had a real chance of sweeping the longtime incumbent congressman right back to wherever he lived, I wasn't the only one captivated. For the media, AOC was a content machine that kept on giving. Every angle was covered— from the signature lipstick (which sold out minutes after she tweeted that it was Stila Stay All Day Liquid Lipstick in the shade Beso) to her DIY grassroots campaign to her personification of what a fed-up generation looked like.

But for me, the true campaign showstopper was AOC's unashamed retelling of her working-class background. Without hesitation, she laid it all out. Her Puerto Rican–born mother worked hard, cleaning toilets, she said, and Ocasio-Cortez did the same when the family was at risk of losing their home after her father died of cancer. She relayed the struggles of young people who wanted, but couldn't afford, a college education. Or families who were barely getting by on minimum wage. During the campaign, we learned, she was a waitress at the type of Manhattan eatery frequented by people who looked like her—other young, thin, and good-looking recent college grads. AOC revealed all this without shame. It was her American story, our American story—*punto y fin*. A story so typical in the boroughs she hoped to represent that it was imperative to mention it.

Her eventual win as the youngest member sworn into Congress was undoubtedly major. That this feat was achieved by a Latina? Even more so. But for me, a Latina who has built a career in mostly white spaces and who's seen many Latina "firsts"—but always from Latinas who didn't share the rest of my life circumstances—AOC's win felt personal. Here was someone who painted her background as an advantage rather than as a sordid secret that had to be buried, the way I'd been burying mine my whole career in the beauty industry.

If you haven't already guessed, I am also Latina. Just how Latina? I own every identifier that matters:

My parents are from the Dominican Republic, but I was born and raised in New York City. Where are they from in the DR? My dad was from Santiago and my mom is from La Romana. Yes, my husband is also Dominican. We share pretty much the same background. He was raised in Washington Heights, and his parents are from Santo Domingo and Santiago. Yes, we both speak Spanish. But our twins don't.

That pretty much sums up my Latina brand. I'm a first-generation American with parents who've been in the United States for over 40 years and whose English is nonetheless limited to "No speaky inglés." On paper, this sounds really strange, but this was the reality for almost everyone in Inwood, the predominantly Dominican neighborhood in uptown Manhattan where I grew up. Our *vecinos* didn't speak English. Neither did the ladies at the 99 cent stores, or the *bodeguero* who sold Mami plantains and frying cheese on credit. Our streets rang with a cacophony of *frio frio* vendors on the corner and Spanish music blasting out of every storefront. Broken English was as good as it was going to get; the rest was augmented with rapid-fire Dominican Spanish. Only the workers at the post office and at the bank and everywhere the adults conducted their business spoke English. And what we were saying to each other in this lively community, set to a merengue beat, was in the language of survival and connection. On summer nights, our building's stoop was our front yard, and the fire hydrants were our water parks. The hoods of the parked cars were the perfect spot to perch, five to a car, and if the owner had rolled down the window and the music was pumping, well, then, even better. Now it's a block party! We never closed our front doors—kids needed easy access when running inside for ice cream truck money.

It was the neighborhood kids, my friends and I, who were the first in our families to master the English language. We had no choice, really, but to surpass our parents.

The bilingual teachers taught mostly kindergarten and first grade. After that, you were shipped off to the English-only classrooms. I don't remember how I made the switch from Spanish to English, but soon, I was speaking both fluently. Maybe too fluently, as my mother would yell at my siblings and me when our English was annoying her. "*Ay! Ese guiri guiri!*" she'd yell, mimicking how the language must've sounded to her foreign ears. "*Hablen español!*" But she also needed this shiny new skill of mine. As the oldest, it was my job—aside from washing down the plastic sofa covers every Saturday morning—to help my parents navigate the mail. And by extension, their lives. Papers were thrust in my face while I was trying to watch *The Love Boat.* I translated letters from the doctor, from the social security office, from the landlord. I was also voted as the Official Caller of Important Offices. And Mami was so impressed with my work that she'd volunteer me to help her friends with their life errands.

My father also took advantage of my beautiful English. (But he paid me with Bustelo and a grateful smile, so he was worth the effort.) I was with him every step of the way when he sought American citizenship. I'll always cherish how much he trusted his interpreter/representative daughter as we marched into the immigration office downtown one afternoon in 1996. His accordion file folder, full of every necessary document, was tucked neatly under his arm. He was ready! What he wasn't expecting was the official's request that I create a travel analysis from Papi's passports. Once I understood the assignment, my father and I barreled down the lunch crowd and settled into a booth at Wendy's. Papi picked up our food while I spread the documents across the table. He watched as I flipped through the little books with the weathered parchment papers and the haphazardly placed stamps. In between sips of my Coke, I made sense of his travels. Papi watched me work, asking questions only when he wouldn't break my concentration. Soon, I was done, and we headed back to the immigration office, our handwritten list safe in the accordion folder.

"Unfortunately," said the official, after a painfully long period reviewing my work, "your dad has spent more time outside of the country than in it. So at this time, we can't move his paperwork forward." My heart sank. You didn't have to speak English to understand that the news wasn't in Papi's favor. I nodded and gave him a reassuring nod. He knew not to interrupt. We were almost out the door when the man called out to me.

"You did a great job with this paperwork," he said. For the first time, he smiled. "In fact, you should consider working here!"

"Thank you, sir," I said with a laugh. I had other plans for myself, but I appreciated the gesture. We said our good-byes and stepped outside. Papi's golden brown eyes opened wide as I explained what the official had said.

"Wait," he said in Spanish. The hallway was crowded but he stopped abruptly to face me. "That man offered you a job in the immigration office of the greatest country in the world?" His hand was clutching my arm.

I had to laugh. He talked about this day for years and

years, a true highlight of his American life. And when he was finally sworn in as a citizen, it was my turn to grin widely as I stood by his side.

There was a lot my parents and I didn't talk about, though. My college ambitions. My dream career. How I'd achieve these dreams. My parents divorced when I was thirteen. The end of their contentious marriage was truly for the best, but it broke my heart to see my proud father move into a tiny room in an apartment nearby. He shared a bathroom with strangers and had to ask permission to make a *cafecito*. Eventually, he returned to the Dominican Republic and remarried and had two more children. He got to bring this new family to New York City, just like he'd done with my mother so many years before.

As much as my mother says she suffered with him, she loves retelling the story that, to her, sums up my father's obsession with his kids: My parents had just brought me home from the hospital. That night she woke to find my father crying over my crib. "*Octavio, que pasó?*" she asked, alarmed. Tearfully, he replied that he feared not seeing me, his first daughter and his first child with my mother, his second wife, grow up.

He was 50 years old then—in our culture, quite old to be a new dad. But in the 23 years that I had him, he made me believe in my potential, almost to an embarrassing degree. He loved everything about me and always told me so. How I navigated the adult world. My perfect English. My ability to discuss *Don Quixote*, which he'd just checked out from the public library around the corner. He told me I was pretty but would follow that with: "Don't let that go to your head." He was beside himself when I got my first job at 14, working with the NYC Summer Youth Program, and helped me secure the photo for my ID card. He also let me know when my actions didn't align with his immigrant beliefs. When I proudly showed off my brand-new credit cards, he frowned and said that it wasn't honorable to be in debt. Deflated, I put them away.

It was my privilege to be at my father's hospital bedside when he passed away at the age of 73. I used my good English to translate his care. Like AOC's father, my father died of lung cancer. And like AOC, I felt like I lost my father when I needed him most.

In the Netflix documentary *Knock Down the House,* viewers got to see Ocasio-Cortez prep for a day on the job. The scenes where she's hauling buckets of ice out of the freezer to get the restaurant where she worked ready for the day so resonated with me. Watching it, I flashed back to myself as a teenager, scrubbing down the pots at the hamburger place at the 34th Street mall food court where I worked. This job was a way to make extra money, nothing more. One day, I found myself explaining this to an older white customer who surprised me by leaning in as I handed her change.

"I hope you're in school," she whispered over the cash register. Taken aback, I replied that yes, of course. I was a junior at JFK High School in the Bronx, I said. I wasn't insulted. Instead, the gesture made me feel like I was worth looking after. Unlike AOC, though, I couldn't make college work. And I tried—twice. The first time, right out of high school, I enrolled in Hunter College, mostly because my neighbor's daughter studied there. I spent a lot of time in my *vecina*'s apartment, blowing out her hair (for fun) and typing her essays (for money), and that was the extent of my vetting process. I don't remember my mother ever asking about my college plans and few of my friends from the block were even considering attending. At Hunter, I was disengaged, discouraged, and struggling to pay tuition. Even with financial aid, my load was more than I could handle. I dropped out before making it to sophomore year.

For my second go-round, I was a little more prepared. By this point I was working as an assistant media planner at an advertising agency in midtown. I was hired as an assistant—and a happy assistant at that. I was an award-winning typist (seriously, I was one of the fastest typists in my high school typing class) and took direction well. I admired my coworkers, even if none of them looked anything like the people back on Dyckman Street. I grew close to my fellow assistants, but sitting in the break room during lunch, watching mind-numbing soap operas, made me realize that I needed to recalibrate. I quickly sought—and got—a promotion and I made an effort to talk to as many people in my growing network as I could about an entirely different industry. The publishing industry. By then, I had started to connect the dots between my abilities, passions, and options. I didn't know any magazine editors but that didn't stop this budding dream from flourishing. I was creating a blueprint to a new American life, so why not aim high? My father had worked in a tire factory and in hotel housekeeping. My mother worked in a tie factory for a minute before my father decided she'd be better off at home. I had nowhere to go but up.

I followed a coworker's advice to look into the Fashion Institute of Technology and enrolled in continuing education courses at night. I was in my element and thriving academically. I barely complained about the long subway ride, at 10 p.m., back home to the Bronx. My new career path was starting to come together, too. Approaching my magazine journalism professor eventually paid off in an editorial assistant position at her magazine. And before long, I'd made my way to *Women's Wear Daily*. But once again, I couldn't afford the college tuition. I decided that my market editor job at *Women's Wear Daily*, the fashion industry bible, was enough schooling for me. And it was free.

Eventually, my ability to channel my immigrant parents' hustle and charisma, combined with my years of striving to be as good as I could be, landed me in top positions in the publishing and beauty worlds. I was always the only Latina at my level at these jobs, which included *W* and *Ladies' Home Journal*, and various communications and creative roles at Lancôme, La Mer, and Bobbi Brown. I learned to contain my Latinidad during the day, happy to unleash it—if only temporarily—when I chatted with the cleaning crew or when the restroom attendants at swanky beauty award luncheons asked me to secure them a goody bag. "*Niña, consigueme una fundita,* please?" Obviously, I obliged.

I kept my Latina side, as defined by the gritty, effervescent women who I grew up around, close to my chest. I dropped my guard a few times, though. Like when I brought my mother to my office at *Ladies' Home Journal.* Mami was visiting from Rhode Island, where she'd eventually moved after the divorce, and she was on a mission to raid the magazine's beauty closet. She was in full-on Mami regalia. A red silk blouse, animal-print leggings, and white Reeboks. Her bleached blond hair was in a skinny ponytail—one less distraction for when she started digging for gold. My sister sat with me in my spacious private office across from the closet. Together, we watched our mother hyperventilate as she shoved beauty products, any beauty products, into her duffel bag. I knew that some were for her own use, but the majority would be shipped back to DR for her sisters.

"You better not let your boss see that," said Irene, barely looking up from the magazine on her lap. "They'll realize you didn't come from money and give you a pay cut." I laughed at the absurdity but was also stung by the truth behind Irene's comment. I yelled out to Mami to chop chop. Let's move this along.

It was when I was named editor of Condé Nast's *Glam Belleza Latina* magazine that I felt my true, fully formed self bloom. Here, I was obligated to be as Latina as possible.

My job depended on it! (Translation: I could blast YouTube videos of Juan Luis Guerra concerts in my office because, guess what? I'm the Latina editor.) I was the most Latina that I'd ever been professionally, but I continued to keep my family's financial struggles and my unique community to myself. I focused more on the quality of my writing and less on the cultural differences between myself and my Condé Nast coworkers. I was determined to bring my highest level of journalism chops to this position. After all, Anna Wintour was my boss's boss.

At *Glam Belleza Latina* I met one accomplished Latina after another. Actresses, models, pop stars, beauty experts, legends. All were impressive and pioneering and living their best Latina lives. As a fan, I was always thrilled to interview them. And as a fellow Latina, I'd consider how I'd speak to them (English? Spanish? Spanglish?) and how I'd get them to share stories that would help me (and my readers) find a piece of myself in them. I understood and loved my privileged position of holding these women, especially those who weren't household names, up to the spotlight.

I relished talking to those Latinas breaking barriers in their respective fields, outside of entertainment, the many Latina "firsts." From education to politics to business, I was always excited to meet Latinas whom I could not only consider role models, but who would hold up a mirror to my own professional experience. But aside from the similar-sounding last name or a shared country of origin, I soon learned that we weren't all created equal. Fairly or not, I judged their journey to success on the advantages that I never experienced. Many of these women had parents who spoke English and who knew how to navigate the nuances of American success. They had college degrees because they were able to secure the funding and the guidance. And money. The idea of money is fairly fluid, but to me, if you had enough money to vacation every summer or to go to camp or to eat at a restaurant that wasn't Burger King, then you had money. In other words, they weren't me.

"Yes," I'd think, "she's a Latina 'first' but she's not like me because . . ."

Until I heard of Alexandria Ocasio-Cortez.

Today, I'm proud to ask my daughter, a college sophomore, if she knows who Ocasio-Cortez is. The flicker of recognition comes quickly. "The woman with the red lipstick? Who's from the Bronx? And the youngest member of Congress?"

Yes, that's the one.

"*Pa'lante!*": The Long History of Puerto Rican Activism in New York City

Pedro A. Regalado

Women of color burst onto the national stage during the 2018 midterm elections, diversifying America's local and national politics. Ilhan Omar, Deb Haaland, and Jahana Hayes were just a few of the candidates whose historic feat helped to shift public conversations to focus boldly on the country's, and indeed the globe's, most marginalized people. In New York, this movement had particular resonance as the enthusiastic Bronx native Alexandria Ocasio-Cortez won one of the most exciting elections in recent memory when she defeated incumbent congressman and Democratic caucus chair Joe Crowley in New York City's 14th congressional district. Crowley had positioned himself to become the next House Democratic leader and hadn't faced a real primary challenge in 14 years, making his defeat at the hands of a first-time candidate in her twenties highly unlikely. When the two met face-to-face, Ocasio-Cortez contended that the district required a representative who reflected its overwhelmingly working-class character: 70 percent of its residents are people of color. As a working-class Latina willing to take on big-money interests, Ocasio-Cortez reckoned she fit the bill.

Since then, Ocasio-Cortez has garnered wide media attention for her progressive positions ranging from her support of the Green New Deal to her controversial stance that immigrant detention centers are concentration camps. Yet, you won't find many mainstream media articles that grapple with the complexity of Ocasio-Cortez's Latina background or how it might contribute to the young politician's engagement with our political culture. This is despite the fact that the congressional district she represents is comprised of nearly 50 percent Latinx residents.

Ocasio-Cortez's heritage matters. Twenty-eight years old when she was elected to Congress, her politics drew on and represented more than just the modern progressive movement or frustration with the status quo and President Trump. She built upon the long history of Latinx political activism in New York, and her victory provides a formula for how the Democratic Party can re-energize itself. That Ocasio-Cortez fights for issues that have universal resonance from a highly particular vantage point—that of a working-class Latina woman from New York—announces to Democrats that they don't need to reinvent the wheel. Instead, her success demonstrates that the Democratic Party's rejuvenation, if it is to have one at all, partially lies in tapping into the voices of those who have been historically neglected but who have fought for today's most pressing social issues. The young leader did not simply embrace the platform of the mainstream progressives. Rather, her victory and those of an array of other women show how the mainstream left is shifting in the direction of policies that Latinx activists, politicians, and everyday people have struggled to achieve for decades.

Waves of Latinx families (including Ocasio's mother) immigrated to New York during the second half of the twentieth century. Between 1940 and 1960 alone, Gotham gained an astonishing 600,000 Puerto Ricans. Puerto Ricans on the island packed up their belongings and left their cities, towns, and often loved ones behind for the promise of a better life in the famed metropolis in the north. The transition was arduous to say the least. In addition to the difficulty of learning a new language—often as adults—Puerto Rican families confronted immediate hardship upon arriving in New York. They faced racial discrimination, a lack of affordable housing, limited access to health care, unequal schooling, and an increasingly stratified job market. Many early migrants during this period found work in New York's manufacturing industry, though they did so just as that sector began to decline as a share of the city's employment.

To make matters worse, New York's political establishment was broadly unwilling to accommodate Puerto Rican migrants' grievances and deliberately marginalized their voices in development decisions impacting their neighborhoods. They did so even as Puerto Ricans increasingly constituted a major part of New York's population. For Puerto Ricans and African Americans alike, the program that we have come to know as "urban renewal" became the central force driving them out of their homes during the midcentury. Enacted through the federal Housing Act of 1949, urban renewal funneled immense financial resources toward public housing and urban redevelopment and invested politicians and city planners across the country with the power to transform neighborhoods. Title I of the law, which took a bulldozer approach to clearing "slums," authorized $1 billion in federal loans to help cities acquire what planners considered "blighted land" for public and private development. In a move difficult to imagine in today's political climate, the federal government guaranteed it would cover two-thirds of the cost.

Though originally intended for the construction of new housing (some of which would purportedly house former residents), amendments to the policy in 1954 eventually enabled the creation of Lincoln Center, nearby Columbus Circle, and many other major development projects in New York City. Puerto Ricans and other Latinx New Yorkers held little sway over the matter. City officials such as planning czar Robert Moses didn't see a place for them, either.

"They expect me to build playgrounds for that scum float-ing up from Puerto Rico," he famously told a colleague. By the late 1960s, urban renewal displaced roughly 30,000 families. Nearly half of them were families of color who were often barred from moving into the segregated white neighborhoods and suburbs that surrounded the city. Since most of these projects took place in the poor neighborhoods of Manhattan and Brooklyn, which were considered slums, many Puerto Rican families migrated across the East River to the South Bronx, where new challenges awaited them during the 1960s and 1970s. In a 1962 report on housing, the Puerto Rican Citizens' Housing Committee, a group of concerned Puerto Ricans, argued that part of the over-all program's goal was "to envision a New York without Puerto Ricans."

During an era when many Americans knew little about the lives of Puerto Rican migrants, middle-class audiences who picked up anthropologist Oscar Lewis's 1966 book, *La Vida: A Puerto Rican Family in the Culture of Poverty— San Juan and New York*, were offered a portrait of a dys-functional family destined for poverty. *La Vida* won a National Book Award, and Lewis's portrayal helped to position Latinx people squarely in the middle of national debates about the roots of poverty and the resources that poor non-whites did or did not deserve. A few years later, in 1970, *Beyond the Melting Pot: The Negroes, Puerto Ricans, Jews, Italians, and Irish of New York City*, by Nathan Glazer and Daniel Patrick Moynihan (author of the controversial report *The Negro Family: The Case for National Action*), concluded that in the twentieth century, Puerto Ricans had been socially and politically inactive compared to some of New York's other prominent ethnic groups. In their account, Puerto Rican community building had not truly existed on the island of Puerto Rico. So how could it possibly translate into political organizing among migrants establishing roots in New York?

Yet, as historian Virginia E. Sánchez Korrol's work demonstrates, Puerto Ricans and other Spanish-speaking New Yorkers had a long history of community organizing in the city. Raised in the South Bronx during the 1950s, Sánchez Korrol remembered learning nothing about her Puerto Rican heritage at her Irish-Catholic school, though her work as a historian later in life excavated the richness of the city's Puerto Rican past. Ultimately, Sánchez Korrol found that the Spanish-speaking postwar newcomers did not, as Glazer and Moynihan's depiction suggested, resign themselves to the dim fates that the urban political landscape offered. Instead, they organized politically, often with other communities, in a range of ways that improved everyday people's lives.

One of the first groups to build on this organizing tradition and combat municipal neglect during the 1960s was Mobilization for Youth (MFY), formed in 1962 by the African American and Puerto Rican mothers of the Lower East Side. MFY emerged just as the Civil Rights movement increased attention to prevailing poverty among African

American and Latinx people. The community social work agency used direct-action politics, including school boycotts and sit-ins at the city welfare department, to demand decent, affordable housing and an end to residential segregation. They also participated in the citywide rent strikes of 1964, drawing Lower East Side residents together across race to advocate for decent living conditions and to keep the city's landlords accountable. These activists, historian Tamar Carroll argues, shaped the national War on Poverty in the process. President Lyndon Johnson's Community Action Programs in 1964 were modeled after MFY's efforts, particularly their commitment to the concept of "maximum feasible participation" on the part of local residents along with the direct influx of federal funds.

New York City's Young Lords Party, established in 1969, became another prominent group in this tradition of Latinx activism. Originally a chapter of the Chicago-based Young Lords Organization and inspired by radical organizations like the Black Panthers, they were comprised of second-generation Puerto Ricans, mostly teenagers and 20-year-olds. The Young Lords challenged the structural poverty that plagued much of urban America during the height of the Civil Rights era with, once again, community-based direct action. In particular, they organized around the rights of New York's Puerto Rican community, whom they believed Mayor John Lindsay's administration had shunned, bringing awareness and change on issues ranging from lead poisoning to neighborhood displacement caused by urban renewal. When Young Lords members forcibly occupied Lincoln Hospital in 1970, they did so because they believed that the Bronx's poor residents deserved basic health care services. As part of their "Ten-Point Health Program" distributed earlier that year, they made their demands loud and clear: "We want 'door-to-door' preventative health services emphasizing environment and sanitation control, nutrition, drug addiction, maternal and child care and senior citizen services."

Before the Young Lords Party disbanded later that decade, members addressed the lack of garbage service in their neighborhoods, organized a free breakfast program, and tested residents for tuberculosis. They often brought about change through shock tactics (e.g., dumping trash in the middle of the street) that disrupted politics as usual. The collective left behind a powerful ideology that championed community pride as well as direct-action politics. This separated them from the famed Latinx politicians of the era who were far less confrontational in their approach, including Herman Badillo, the first Puerto Rican elected to the House of Representatives. To be sure, Badillo became a highly trusted figure among Latinx New Yorkers by 1980. But as he advanced his career, Badillo's political turn rightward alienated him from those within the progressive left as well as mainstream Puerto Rican political leadership.

Ocasio-Cortez is too young to have experienced these foundational moments of the Civil Rights era of Latinx

New York. She wasn't around when television announcers gestured to the intense flames in the South Bronx that provided the backdrop for the 1977 World Series. Nor did she witness the lethal outcomes of the 1980s drug wars, which generated shockingly high murder rates and levels of street violence that made New York's poor black and Latinx neighborhoods among the most dangerous in the country. Still, Ocasio-Cortez is a product of this history and, most importantly, the variety of Latinx responses to it. Tactically somewhere between organizations like MFY, the Young Lords, and politicians like Badillo, her fusion of the distinct tools of Latinx activism, including outspoken in-your-face politics, working-class participation, and Latinx pride, with those of the wider progressive movement, such as her identification as a democratic socialist, her door-to-door campaign, and her public recognition that black and LGBTQ+ lives matter, provides her and her colleagues opportunities that earlier leaders did not have. Affordable housing, fair wages, and universal health care are increasingly becoming viable centerpieces of the Democratic platform in ways that might have amazed previous generations of Latinx activists.

Some critics, political scientist Mark Lilla the most prominent among them, argue that organizing from a vantage point of racial or cultural particularity fails to generate the appeal necessary to keep Democrats, and progressives more generally, in office. Lilla, the author of *The Once and*

Future Liberal: After Identity Politics, maintains that social movements and party politics are at odds. Ocasio-Cortez's success tells us otherwise. Through her advocacy, she has shown how her experiences as a Puerto Rican woman from a working-class background (a designation that those on the political right and moderates alike often reserve for low-income whites) can deepen the Democratic Party's understanding of the problems that continue to plague non-white and other poor Americans while providing a toolkit with which to tackle them.

Like her predecessors, Ocasio-Cortez's brand of political organizing responds to this generation's set of social challenges. She is upfront about how the issues that have shaped her own life as a Latinx woman, and that have led her to seek office, affect more and more people across the nation. While the urban renewal projects referenced above were a major force of displacement some 60 years ago, gentrification poses one of the greatest threats to urban communities of color today. Housing insecurity in high-rent cities like New York and San Francisco also negatively impacts income-stagnant, loan-burdened young people more broadly. Ocasio-Cortez's struggles to secure affordable housing in D.C. made her a target for right-wing media outlets, but such a basic struggle actually resonates deeply with her generation. Today's young adults know all too well the stark income inequality that has only deepened since the Civil Rights era. About 20 percent of New York's residents lived below the poverty line in 1980, just five years after Gotham nearly went bankrupt. In 2017, that figure stood at about 19 percent.

Amid this crisis of economic disparity, Nuyoricans are joined by migrants from the Dominican Republic, Mexico, El Salvador, Colombia, and elsewhere. Together, Latinx people amount to about 2.5 million of New York City's residents, roughly a third of the city. About a quarter of them were poor in 2016. The case is similar with Latinx people nationally, who now number upward of 59 million (or 18 percent of the population). For many, unauthorized status—and containment at the border—forces them to question the moral underpinnings of this nation's immigration apparatus. Indeed, the issues Ocasio-Cortez and her peers fight for are of utmost urgency. Their stakes as high as ever.

It's hard to imagine that Ocasio-Cortez could have anticipated years back, when she and her family struggled financially, that she would come to speak for a generation. In a January 2019 Instagram post that pictured the young politician's swearing-in alongside her mother, Ocasio-Cortez wrote, "It wasn't long ago that we felt our lives were over; that there were only so many do-overs until it was just too late, or too much to take, or we were too spiritually spent." Since then, the national political landscape has only grown more contentious as both sides of the partisan spectrum seek to build momentum leading into November 2020. U.S. House and Senate challengers increasingly include outsiders and experienced politicians alike; they are community organizers, lawyers, and, like Ocasio-Cortez, first-time candidates committed to bold progressive ideas.

It seems, thus, that Ocasio-Cortez's tenure is both part of a trend toward the re-emergence of working-class progressive politics, as well as a potent Latinx symbol of it. Tough days undoubtedly lie ahead for Ocasio-Cortez, but she can draw strength and inspiration from the social movements of Latinx New Yorkers who have worked over the past 60 years to bring the myriad issues affecting the city's poor communities to the fore. During our own moment of political turbulence, her words and deeds embody the Young Lords' courageous call from half a century ago: "*Pa'lante!*"

The Imagined Threat of a Woman Who Governs Like a Man

Rebecca Traister

In December 2018, weeks before Alexandria Ocasio-Cortez was even sworn into office, the online magazine *Politico* posted a provocative, anonymously sourced piece claiming that the New York congresswoman-elect might be planning, in concert with Justice Democrats, to recruit a Democratic primary challenger to her fellow New York congressman Hakeem Jeffries in 2020, in part in response to his undercutting of California congresswoman and progressive stalwart Barbara Lee in a November House leadership election. Ocasio-Cortez later dismissed the piece, calling it "birdcage lining."

However inaccurate the facts in *Politico*'s reporting may have been, the piece was useful and telling—the expression of a building fever dream about Ocasio-Cortez, and the fears of what she might be capable of, should she continue to flash her unprecedented willingness to make bold demands and push her party where she thinks it should go. Ocasio-Cortez's eagerness to flex her muscles, without demurring or waiting for her turn—without even waiting to be sworn in—is undergirding nightmarish fears about her as an agent of chaos and destruction. The *Politico* story itself was illustrated with an image of the Bronx native appearing to literally rub her hands together while grinning like Dr. Evil.

Reading the piece, I couldn't help but think of Naomi Alderman's brain-bending novel, *The Power*, published in 2016. It depicts a world in which women develop the power to inflict physical pain, and to kill, via electricity that emanates from their fingers. In Alderman's fictional universe, this power is exhibited first by young women, who in turn awaken it in their elders; as they are learning the possibilities and limits of their new power, the women giddily experiment with it, sending sparks and currents, determining how much of it they have, whether they can control it, and how they might best deploy it.

The book is extraordinary because it forces readers to think about all the ways—within our social, sexual, professional, and political relationships—in which men's power over women is so much taken for granted that we don't question it, don't even notice it. But when women acquire an equivalent force, chaos and fear reign. *The Power* read to many and was regularly reviewed as a piece of chilling dystopian fiction. But as Alderman herself has said, "It's only a dystopia for the men . . . nothing happens to a man in this book that is not happening right now to a woman somewhere in the world."

What the reaction to Ocasio-Cortez makes undeniable is that if and when women gain enough power to start behaving, in a political sphere, as men have for so long, they will be viewed with fright and discomfort.

Jeffries, a popular incumbent who is generally (though not universally) well regarded by progressives, supposedly wound up in Ocasio-Cortez's crosshairs in part because of his own tactical moves, which reportedly helped gain him a House leadership position.

In October 2018, he jumped into the race against Lee for Democratic caucus chair just a few weeks before the midterm elections. Lee was hoping to become the first African American woman in history to serve in party leadership. According to *The Intercept*, she believed that she had the votes, but Jeffries was helped at the last minute by one of his mentors, Joe Crowley, the long-serving New York congressman who'd been beaten in his June primary race by Ocasio-Cortez. Crowley reportedly falsely intimated to caucus members that Lee had donated to Ocasio-Cortez in advance of the primary, depicting her as supportive of the insurgent spirit Ocasio-Cortez has come to symbolize. Some of the votes Lee thought she had locked down changed, and Jeffries won the caucus chair slot by ten votes.

The piece suggesting that Ocasio-Cortez—angry at having been used to defeat a woman she admires by a man she beat— might want to oust Jeffries prompted an affronted response.

"Can we call this out for being dumb?" Bakari Sellers tweeted, calling Jeffries "one of our most talented members." The actor Jeffrey Wright gravely noted that "quick fame is a funny thing," apparently in reference to Ocasio-Cortez, and the columnist Michael Cohen predicted that Ocasio-Cortez was going to "wear out her welcome very quickly."

In some ways, the strong defense of Jeffries wasn't surprising. He's extremely popular in his district, belongs to the Progressive Caucus, and is widely understood to have ambitions to succeed Nancy Pelosi as his party's leader and become the country's first black Speaker of the House. Jeffries may be a lovely man and a decent progressive, but it is also true that in his efforts to gain leadership of his party, he relied on a network of old-school male power (a network invested in its own form of revenge) to defeat a beloved and ideologically unimpeachable woman. No, this isn't a capital offense; it's not a shock; it is, in fact, just politics—what happens every day, not just in Congress but in workplaces around the country.

It happens in part because networks of power are built by and around men, especially white men. To the extent that they permit the entrance of those who are not white men, it is often black men (like Jeffries) and white women who are admitted and supported. But Lee is a black woman who was running for a leadership position in a party that relies on black women's votes and electoral and activist labor yet rarely acknowledges, let alone endorses, their authority by electing them to positions of leadership.

There has historically been little cost to undercutting women of color on your way to power, because neither white women nor black men have had the power or the inclination to stand up for them in the way, for example, that Crowley and his supporters are alleged to have done for Jeffries in his leadership bid. And also because, hey—once you have the power, you have the power; who's going to come for you once you ascend?

The tantalizing (or terrifying) possibility laid out in this small—overstated, perhaps even fantasized—story about Ocasio-Cortez coming for Jeffries was that we could, perhaps, imagine these dynamics changing, and that is shocking. Naturally, Ocasio-Cortez would be livid if a falsehood related to her campaign, allegedly propagated by the man she beat, were used to defeat an admired potential mentor. What's arresting is the notion that she might be in a position—might have enough swagger and sway—to imagine doing something in response. That long-powerful men like Crowley might deploy a vengeful fuck-you isn't a shocking notion . . . but what if newly powerful women could conceive of doing the same?

It's this very possibility that's exhilarating for some, chilling for others: that women, and in this case, progressive women of color, newly elected in historic numbers, might team up in defense of one another, come to each other's aid, exact political revenge on those who would vanquish their allies in ways they have never been capable of before. Because it's not that women in the past haven't had the will or desire to respond to the affront of having been stepped over by powerful men; it's that they have not had the numbers, the voice, or the chutzpah that comes with those things until very, very recently. What's scary to so many about Ocasio-Cortez is that she's acting like a politician with power.

And apparently, that provokes an almost primal fear. Like *The Power*, like the #MeToo movement, like the rising activism of women around the country in the years since Donald Trump's victory, this story elicited a kind of shiver down the spine. We live in a world in which some people are used to being able to ascend without obstacle, without recrimination, without challenge: What if, suddenly, that changed? What if men were taken to task for sidelining or kneecapping women on their way to greater power? What if there was a price to be paid?

There's zero evidence that a challenge to Jeffries will become a reality, much less that it's a top priority for Ocasio-Cortez, who has disavowed the story and whose hands are very full with being the Democratic Party's fastest-rising star and pushing her party to get behind a Green New Deal, and who—not for nothing—would indeed take an enormous risk in going after one of the party's favorite sons.

But there was something downright electrifying about seeing how uncomfortable it made so many people to even imagine a young politician testing out her power in this way—the giddy, exhilarating thrill of watching those sparks fly.

In No Uncertain Terms

Natalia Sylvester

My parents refused to let my sister and me forget how to speak Spanish by pretending they didn't understand when we spoke English. Spanish was the only language we were allowed to speak in our one-bedroom apartment in Miami in the late 1980s. We both graduated from English-as-a-second-language lessons in record time as kindergartners and first graders, and we longed to play and talk and live in English, as if it were a shiny new toy.

"No te entiendo," my mother would say, shaking her head and shrugging in feigned confusion anytime we slipped into English. My sister and I would let out exasperated sighs at having to repeat ourselves in Spanish, only to be interrupted by a correction of our grammar and vocabulary after every other word. "One day you'll thank me," my mother would retort.

I used to picture this "one day" in a far-off future. I'd

imagine myself going back to my birth country of Peru and being mistaken for a local. I'd daydream about my perfect Spanish being the deciding factor in my nailing a difficult job interview.

What I couldn't have known is that my Spanish was never fated to be perfect. How could it be, when English was the main vehicle through which I consumed everything? It was the language of my friends, my teachers, my textbooks, and the movies, TV shows, songs, and stories I loved. To counter our complete immersion, my mother began asking friends who visited Peru to bring back history and grammar books for my sister and me. We'd come home from school only to have additional lesson plans laid out for us on my parents' bedspread.

En esta casa se habla español.

But when you speak your first language only at home, it becomes your second. It becomes the carrier of all things domestic, its development stunted like a grown child who never makes it out on their own.

Which is why, the first time I heard AOC speak Spanish on national television, I experienced pride, horror, shame, joy, and relief all in the time it took her to form one sentence. It was for an interview she'd done on Univision, and on Twitter she shared it along with an acknowledgment that, "Growing up, Spanish was my first language— but like many 1st generation Latinx Americans, I have to continuously work at it & improve. It's not perfect, but the only way we improve our language skills is through public practice."

In the three-minute clip, before she'd said a word, I heard a voiceover of Univision anchor Yisel Tejeda. Her vowels were crisp and enunciated. Her accent was ambiguous enough to be from any and all Latin American countries. Her vocabulary was formal, effortless, and precise.

It created a sharp contrast to AOC's form of speech. Listening to her talk about the Green New Deal, I found myself taking mental notes of her slight errors in the conjugations of her words, wincing when her plural nouns didn't match up with her singular verbs. When she paused longer than expected midsentence, I knew it was because she was translating in her mind, searching for the right word. I recognized the silence, the moment when you realize certain words have escaped you, and you have to make do with the ones you have. Her accent, laced with the most subtle traces of English, reminded me of my own.

In that moment I felt embarrassed for her, embarrassed for myself. To deal with the shame of hearing my own flawed Spanish come out of someone else's mouth, I first reached for the cheapest of coping mechanisms, comparing and critiquing AOC's fluency. How easily we perpetuate internalized harm, especially if we've never stopped to interrogate its roots.

Then Tejeda asked AOC about her calling Trump a racist. "On what do you base those claims?"

Unshaken, AOC responded, "He is very clear in his treatment, his words, and his actions." She went on to describe his tactics of intimidating our community and ended by saying "Él tiene intención a dar miedo de nuestras comunidades, pero no podemos dar él el poder de hacer eso."

If someone wanted to, they could translate this sentence back to English in all its errors and awkwardness, but that would be a disservice to its meaning, its heart, its conviction. Perfect words or not, AOC is unafraid to speak in no uncertain terms on the things that matter most. She calls out racism and this president's intentions to stoke fear against our communities. We cannot give him the power to do that.

In 2014, when my first book, *Chasing the Sun*, was published, a reporter at my local Univision station invited me to promote the novel on their morning show. I was in a panic for days leading up to it. At night, I'd call my mom and rehearse what I'd say and how I'd say it. I'd tell her an entire sentence in English, and she'd repeat it back to me in Spanish while I wrote it down. It's not that I didn't know how to say these things; it's just that I didn't think my way of saying them was good enough. Spanish was my language for everyday things—words that spoke of food and packing for trips and missing aunts and uncles the few times we spoke on the phone. The words I needed to discuss my book's themes and characters felt tucked away somewhere unreachable to me. They were literary words. High-concept words. Not home words and heart words.

So I created a script that allowed me to play the part of a perfectly bilingual Latina. I memorized every line. When the reporter emailed me to confirm our interview time, I wrote back using my iPhone, which has a trusty Spanish keyboard that autocorrects my misplaced tildes and spelling errors before I can even make them. Heaven forbid I leave out a silent *h* or add an accent where it didn't belong.

What would people think?

What I should have been asking: Where does this deep-seated humiliation come from?

We didn't always call it español in my family. I remember my grandmother, in particular, faithfully calling what we spoke castellano. While literally both these words mean Spanish, one of them more explicitly ties the language back to its roots in the Castilla region of Spain. Growing up, I thought of these words as synonymous, but like all words, their meanings have power and purpose. That their difference is implied is what makes it all the more dangerous. People in Latin America and the United States speak español, and in fact each region makes it their own with specific words, phrases, and dialects that make it sound different from European Spanish. But we spoke castellano, the original, proper version blessed and validated by the

Real Academia Española. Never mind that our vocabularies and cadences are distinctly Peruvian, that we sound nothing like actual Spaniards.

My family wanted to believe that we spoke Good Spanish because to speak it any other way would make us sound less educated. Less cultured. Less worthy. I didn't realize it at the time, but this insistence on linguistic purity is steeped in centuries of colonization and classism. Imported from our family's own birth countries to this one, it only serves to perpetuate the belief that Latinx immigrants must be white adjacent, white pleasing, in order to be accepted. It replicates hierarchical social structures that look down on the working class and assign superiority to those in possession of more wealth, education, and power.

In other words, it represents everything AOC stands against.

The documentary *Knock Down the House* opens with Ocasio-Cortez scooping barrels of ice during her job as a bartender. In her off hours, she takes to the streets, handing out flyers to residents of the Bronx. She speaks to them in English, Spanish, and bits of Bengali. "Over 200 languages are spoken in my district of NY-14," she's tweeted. "I can speak 4 (2 are rusty, but it's like a bike)."

As a working-class woman of color, AOC's willingness to speak—and embrace—the language of the working-class immigrant families she represents is game changing. It is arguably one of the main reasons she got elected, and now that she has power, she is changing our perception not just of what a powerful Latina looks and sounds like, but of the people whose interests are being served in the White House.

"Estamos aqui por usted," she says in the Univision interview, speaking to the Bronx community and specifying that this included its undocumented residents. *We are here for you.*

In July 2019, Yazmin Juárez—a Guatemalan asylum seeker whose 19-month-old daughter, Mariee, died shortly after being released from ICE custody—testified in front of the House Oversight subcommittee to denounce the cruelty and neglect she experienced while in detention. In Spanish translated by an interpreter, Juárez told the subcommittee, "The world should know what is happening to so many children inside these ICE detention facilities."

Among the members of Congress who listened to and questioned Juárez was AOC. She opened her statement by speaking directly to Juárez and thanking her, in Spanish, for her bravery in sharing her story. She paused before continuing, clearly overcome with emotion. She briefly switched to English, uttering, "I don't—," then seemed to change her mind. Whatever Ocasio-Cortez meant to say in that moment, she couldn't bring herself to find the words.

Instead, she cleared her throat and began her questioning. At times, she looked down at what were probably notes, carefully scripted sentences in Spanish. She spoke of policy and law—using phrases like requiere y mantengan—to iterate that U.S. law requires children held in ICE custody to be kept in safe and sanitary conditions. Her tone was firm and clear, but it also carried a softness, a palpable compassion directed at a grieving mother as Ocasio-Cortez turned her statement into a question: *In your opinion, were you and your baby here under safe and sanitary conditions?*

Su hija, su bebe, she said. Home words. Heart words.

No, Juárez responded, no.

There are those who'd say that AOC is giving voice to the voiceless, but I disagree. Undocumented immigrants and asylum seekers have a voice, but there are too many people unwilling to listen. Rather than speak for anyone, Ocasio-Cortez has, time and again, used her power and position to amplify their voices. She's taken up and held space so that others may join her in it. When, if ever, has a congressperson sat at that desk and spoken into the mic with imperfect, first-gen–immigrant, working-class Spanish and listened to the untranslated words of a young Latina mother who sacrificed everything for a chance to better her child's life? It means something that a U.S. congresswoman and a Guatemalan asylum seeker could communicate on such a platform without the need for an interpreter. It's powerful to know that the pieces of ourselves too often lost in translation have an ally who will fight for them.

"Did you witness, with your own eyes, a culture of terror within these facilities?" AOC asked next, her voice breaking from trying to hold back tears.

Juárez responded: "When I was in detention in the cages, they interviewed us by phone with the ICE officers. But they wouldn't let us speak. He said to me, with these words: you know that this is a country for Americans, that my president is Donald Trump, and that we can take away your daughter and put you in jail."

There's a question Ocasio-Cortez asks in an interview filmed during the early months of her campaign that I haven't been able to stop thinking about. It's for local NY1 Noticias, a conversation she self-deprecatingly shared on Twitter by joking that she's "Getting my 1st gen bilingual game up one interview at a time . . ."

She struggles as usual. At times, the man interviewing her generously finishes her sentence for her. Sometimes he offers up a word, much in the same way my mom does when we speak on the phone and my mind starts to blank. AOC, like me, takes these bits of aid and keeps going.

But when she's asked about her opponent in the race, Joe Crowley, she easily responds by saying, *What is the point of all that power if it's not going to be used to help working-class families?*

If language is power, then my Spanish, flawed as it may be, has served its purpose by allowing me to help others.

There was the young mother who wanted to know if she could place a diaper bin on hold at the register at Goodwill. The cashier shook her head dismissively and said she didn't understand. It wasn't difficult to read the woman's gestures—she was struggling to push her baby's carriage while lugging the large box around the store. Even after I translated, the cashier's irritation was palpable. The air of judgment is one I've come to recognize, tossed in two directions: how dare this woman not speak English, how dare this other woman speak both English and Spanish.

"Siri, show me the brand of 'economic anxiety' that mocks Americans of color as unintelligent + unskilled, while *also* mocking those same Americans for speaking more languages than you," AOC once tweeted. She was responding to Fox News' Laura Ingraham, who on her show with guest Joseph diGenova had mocked the way Ocasio-Cortez pronounces her own name. "She does the Latina thing," diGenova added, which apparently meant daring to say her name the way it was given to her.

It shouldn't be surprising that a culture founded on genocide and forced assimilation would consider a woman of color's refusal to mispronounce her own name for white people's benefit an act of defiance. Americans who demand every name be made easy for them resent the bit of effort it takes to just listen harder. They feel entitled to a comfort made possible only by oppressing others.

The brand of "economic anxiety" that AOC refers to is, of course, not at all about economics and entirely about race. It is not even unique to our time. Go back one generation, and you'll hear stories of people like my in-laws, whose teachers in Florida beat them for speaking in school the language they spoke at home. Go back yet another generation and you'll hear of the state-sanctioned racial terror inflicted on residents of Mexican descent in Texas in the late 1800s and early 1900s.

On videos circulating on social media you'll hear Americans harassing Spanish speakers at supermarkets and restaurants. This language of xenophobia and white supremacy is spoken fluently by our own president. In July 2019, Trump lashed out at representatives Ilhan Omar of Minnesota, Ayanna Pressley of Massachusetts, Rashida Tlaib of Michigan, and Ocasio-Cortez (the group of freshmen congresswomen known as the squad) by saying that they should "go back and help fix" the countries they came from.

" 'Go back to your own country,' is hallmark language of white supremacists," AOC responded.

It is at the root of why generations of Latinx Americans' relationship with Spanish is laced with pain. Those whose parents tried to shield them from discrimination by not passing it on are often expected to be fluent in a language they never had the chance to forget. Those of us who managed to hold on to it, despite the pressures to assimilate, know that our imperfect Spanish is a privilege we are often shamed for both inside and outside of our communities.

And those of us who speak only Spanish are too often dismissed and, worse, targeted—by women pushing shopping carts, by ICE raids, by gunmen with anti-immigrant manifestos. Their terror makes victims of us all.

A few weeks before the election in 2016, I was at a Walmart parking lot in Manor, Texas, helping register voters. A woman ran to our tent in tears because her car had been stolen. She was crying out for help in Spanish, but in a town with a population that's nearly 50 percent Latinx, none of the cops on site could understand her. As she filed her police report with me as an interpreter, she confided in me that all her papers had been in the car.

How do you translate fear to those you cannot trust?

I've watched the video of AOC on Univision 5, 10, 15 times. It occurs to me that I've been leaving myself out of too many conversations out of fear, and I think maybe if I watch her closely enough, I'll learn how to speak Spanish with more confidence.

In it, there's no room for AOC to overthink or rehearse her answers, and even more impressively: it doesn't matter. When she approaches someone on a sidewalk to talk about the 2020 census, they respond to her warmth and passion, not her grammar. When Tejeda asks her about her favorite food and AOC says, "Mofongo, soy puertorriqueña," the two Latinas laugh in mutual celebration of their community.

There's no challenge to her identity, no doubt cast over her worth. Her Spanish is not flawed, it is simply honest, a more true representation of what it can mean to be first-gen Latinx in the United States today. Rooted in one place and now grounded in another, we find we are constantly translating, journeying back and forth. We find that our language, and the stories it carries, is not a straight path. Not necessarily English or "proper" Spanish or even Spanglish. Not the right words or the wrong words, either.

Here, in the conversations that those like AOC are creating, we don't need to apologize for our language. We have the words we learned at home, the ones we know by heart. They are good enough, powerful enough. They will be heard.

The Center Will Not Hold. Alexandria Ocasio-Cortez Is Counting On It

Erin Aubry Kaplan

First of all, she danced. That's what got my attention, lit a hope for the first time in many months that things were not quite as dire in the country as they seemed. Somebody had unearthed an old 2010 video in which newly elected congresswoman Alexandria Ocasio-Cortez, then a student at Boston University, is seen dancing with fellow students in a spirited sendup of the iconic dance sequence in the 1980s movie *The Breakfast Club*. Every student in the video has a role to play, and Ocasio-Cortez's seems to be one of joy and release; on a city rooftop she boogies and twirls, at one point is on her hands and knees whipping her long, dark hair over her head with abandon. Through it all she smiles big, laughs, clearly reveling in the performance. The video was circulated by a critic as proof that Ocasio-Cortez, a staunch progressive, was a "nitwit" from way back who didn't have the gravitas to serve in Congress.

Her response was not to disavow the video or chalk it up to youthful indiscretion, but to dance some more. She posted an online clip of her boogeying into her new congressional office, doing more subtle moves than she had done nine years earlier, but with unmistakable élan and with that big smile that invited the world in, even the critics. But the message was clear: this dance floor is mine. It was exactly how I often fantasized responding to attacks on my writing by conservatives and dissenters, not with more words, but with dancing. Here was Ocasio-Cortez meeting energy with energy, dispersing the bad energy with her assured grooving like a Jedi laser. My kind of woman. Certainly my kind of politician.

When AOC was elected to Congress in 2017, as the nuclear-winter darkness that is Donald Trump was descending rapidly upon the nation, those of us who were moving very close to despair were jolted back into remembering that there can be light. Light as in a worthy person seeking office can actually win it, light as in the majority of Americans who feel run over by the Trumpocalypse and who have been run over by the Republicans for many years still have a say, still matter despite the vicious belittlement of progressives that's been going on for decades now. Ocasio-Cortez made us remember who we are because of who she is: she's not simply a person worthy of being elected—bright, informed, empathetic, people oriented.

She comprises all the demographics we need to see more of in government right now: female, Latina, of color, young, concerned about climate change and all the other big, paralyzing crises that have piled up over years and are bearing down on all of us, whatever our demographic. In the version of the near future that puts America on a fast train to ruin, unwilling or unable to break the momentum of any big crises, she is a road sign that says: turn here.

Ocasio-Cortez brings not only light, but fire. She wants to do. She is so far most famous for wanting to do something about climate change, not merely be concerned about it as so many of us are. She has an organizer's passion for action, something like Barack Obama in his younger days in Chicago, but unlike Obama she is not concerned with finding solutions to big-scale problems on which everyone can agree; in a post-consensus country, she leads with solutions designed to do nothing less than restore us to—or establish for the first time—a moral and ethical center; it is the only thing that can save us from our own worst impulses, our soft cowardice, and our inertia. In this context it is impossible not to see Ocasio-Cortez as a kind of superheroine; the extraordinary historical moment demands a crusader straight out of a Marvel Studios movie script. It helps that the telegenic, charismatic Ocasio-Cortez could actually star in such a movie, if she weren't in Congress (she was a bartender not long ago, and bartenders get discovered all the time). Between her straightforward ambition to save America and America's well-honed tendency to make heroes and villains out of politicians—the villains these days generally being the dreaded socialists—Ocasio-Cortez couldn't help but be a symbol of comic book proportions, almost from the moment she got elected in a spectacular surprise win over a white male opponent who was so sure he had her beat, he declined to debate her during the campaign. We are used to things being described as "polarizing," but she has electrified the concept. *Time* magazine dubbed her "America's newest human Rorschach test," who has quickly become "the second most talked-about politician in America, after the President of the United States."

This is not as reductive as it sounds. Of course it's distressing—though entirely unsurprising—that Ocasio-Cortez has become the chief bogeywoman for the right; she loudly articulates all the demands of social equality that the right has always feared and loathed. But she is also a much-needed superheroine for everyone else, from centrist Democrats to traditional but unsatisfied Democrats to serious progressives to independents, all of whom are looking to connect to some energy and life—chi, if you will—that's been missing from the party and from the left for a long time. They have all been looking for someone to argue for change with something besides statistics and percentages, because we all know that even the most damning stats, while we can agree that they're awful, don't motivate. Looking for, yes, that almost cultish leader in a party that has always preferred rationality to emotion, mostly because Democrats as a pluralistic party of blacks, immigrants, LGBTQ+, and other defined political groups could never agree on what emotion to feel. We talk a lot about how there are many competing agendas within the party and how that obstructs unity, but what's always been more important are the competing feelings about America it-self—do we like it or not? What do we expect of it? How much of it do we forgive, how much of it do we hold to account?

It gets complicated because feelings about America vary by people's experience, which means they vary by race: whites feel differently about the country than blacks. Those are the biggest cracks that run underneath commonalities of class and sexual orientation and gender that look solid on paper, commonalities the Democrats like to highlight because addressing racial difference—to say nothing of emotional difference rooted in race—is too challenging to the white leadership of the party, as it is to most white people. In their view it doesn't engender hope and unity, but the opposite. Good intentions notwithstanding, this is an ahistorical privileged view of the central role of color (which begins with white tribalism) that has doomed us to keep repeating the mistake of hewing to some superficial and bloodless idea of unity that nobody really buys. In this vacuum of emotional conviction, Democrats have drifted ever closer to Republican values and practices—deregulat-ing banks, dismantling welfare, trumpeting law and order.

AOC infuses this bloodlessness with the truth about color, and with her own unapologetically passionate feelings about America. She brings new life to the Democrats, and to Congress, as a woman of color who understands all of its permutations in American life because she has lived that life. Contrary to the tired old political shibboleth that race polarizes, her experience as a person of color has made her not polarizing or divisive but incredibly idealistic and hopeful. She says she joined the Democratic Socialists of America because it was the rare organization that saw the country, and its potential for a Great Society, as fully as she did. "Every time I was joining my brothers and sisters in the Movement for Black Lives, DSA was there," she told *Vogue* magazine.

When I saw these actions, it was like, Okay, this is clearly an extension of our own community. And the thing about DSA is that it's a very large tent organization. When we talk about the word socialism, I think what it really means is just democratic participation in our economic dignity, and our economic, social, and racial dignity . . . To me, what socialism means is to guarantee a basic level of dignity. It's asserting the value of saying that the America we want and the America that we are proud of is one in which all children can access a dignified education. It's one in which no person is too poor to have the medicines they need to live. It's to say that no individual's civil rights are to be violated. And it's also to say that we need to really examine the historical inequities that have created much of the inequalities—both in terms of economics and social and racial justice—because they are intertwined. This idea of, like, race or class is a false choice.

Martin Luther King Jr. himself couldn't have said it better. But he paid a price for his passion: toward the end of his life, as he identified more and more as a socialist, he became less and less popular with mainstream politicians and other leaders who were willing to support civil rights, but not a larger vision of ensuring equality and access for all. King died without realizing his ultimate dream, but it lived on—orphaned by both political parties for decades but sustained by individuals and organizations ranging from the Revolutionary Communist Party to the Reverend William Barber in North Carolina. AOC is bringing that radical vision to the floor of Congress, and not a moment too soon. Whether it is realized is up to the people, but what is clear is that it must first be brought.

AOC calls herself black and Puerto Rican, which is refreshing and important. When it comes to identity, black Latinos tend to choose nation over race, not least because blackness in the United States isn't exactly advantageous. If you're a political or public figure, being black automatically puts you in the crosshairs of conservatives, who are always triggered by race (Obama, anyone?). Puerto Ricans are American and are often black, though they tend not to identify as either; AOC brings Puerto Rican, black, and American together in the same space, where they rightly belong. Her embrace of color is doubtless a big reason why the right resents her so deeply, why there are MABA shirts (Make Alexandria a Bartender Again, featuring AOC with a pinched, unappealing face) to augment the ugly racial resentment first put forth and still sustained by MAGA. AOC goes straight into that maw by making not just the needs, but the feelings of people of color a central part of her agenda, as well as an integral part of truth, justice, and the American way. For her, color is not something to strategically market or constantly modify, as Obama was forced to do. It is not anti-American, but the opposite. In a larger sense she knows (as I hope we all do by now) that staying in the center, or "neutral," racially or otherwise, is not the answer to anything, certainly not to the problem of emotional paralysis that has truly unmade the Democratic Party.

The *New Yorker* acknowledged the potential of AOC's emotional power when it noted during her 2018 congressional run, "Her campaign managed to channel the full range of progressive alarm." It later noted how that alarm has translated into the more intimate, ordinary-person-as-celebrity power of social media, which has made AOC a bona fide star. "No lawmaker in recent memory has translated so few votes into so much political and social capital so quickly," the magazine noted. "Her Twitter following has climbed from about 49,000 last summer to more than 3.5 million. Thousands of people tune in to watch her make black-bean soup or re-pot her houseplants on Instagram Live. Immediately after she tweeted the name of her signature red lipstick—Beso, by Stila—it sold out online."

I love the red lipstick—it's as cheerily visceral a rejoinder to the naysayers as the dancing, an acknowledgment of AOC's self-confidence and style, not to mention her sense of play. It is power. I frankly love the fact that she's still in her club-hopping years and that she is so vibrant and beautiful and still forming. She reminds us all, especially women, of that feeling that simply being young and emergent is force enough to change the world, or enough to have a shot at changing it. We all need to see the world change, we all need to channel AOC, not just young folk most adept at social media. Though admittedly, it's the millennials and generation Zers who are most in need of a blueprint and a beacon. AOC was born in 1989. The greed-is-good boom of the decade was passing, Reaganomics was already shoring up the 99 percent, and a crippling recession and explosion of mass incarceration lay just over the horizon. AOC has said that she never saw American prosperity in her life. She can't live on the same memories of the sixties and seventies many of us live on, or console ourselves with, or make the foundation of our denial. Make America Great Again is truly just a slogan to her generation, an idea that's not just wrong but nonexistent.

The lack of a living connection to the real fruits of American promise is having consequences, chiefly that an acceptance of socialism is rising among the young. A frequently cited Harvard poll shows that young people are embracing democratic socialism more and more, tacking more and more left on practically every issue. AOC is part of this shift. Before running for Congress she struggled with student debt and worked multiple jobs to stave off the foreclosure of her family home. As a politician she is advocating for herself, which by definition means advocating for system change. She is not a wealthy or privileged person looking to accrue more money and power, like Trump—she has nothing to accrue to. She sees enrichment in a completely different way, to be used for a different purpose. She is redefining the meaning of *self-interest*, enlightening it in a way it hasn't been enlightened since the New Deal. It's no accident that her first big policy proposal—one that addresses all those progressive alarms, from climate change to job creation to racial justice—is named after FDR's own signature legislation, which aimed not just at reining in banks but at recasting a broken and immoral system. Except that AOC's Green New Deal does not exclude blacks or women or the poor, as the original New Deal did. This is truly new, and long overdue. Its time has come.

Of course, not all Democrats are on board with AOC. The centrists see her as a kind of bullet that explodes, shredding a target from the inside. "America isn't her district," warned Joel Benenson, a Democratic advisor who believes that the party can't prosper without the support of core moderates and centrists. "Democrats shouldn't take the bait." Bait? It makes AOC sound like a Trojan horse, rolling into our fortress to trick us into embracing big change, only to have the gift blow up in our faces. Except that it's caution and constantly legitimizing the hysteria of the right that has blown up in Democrats' faces and left them figuring out how to fight, and who to lead a fight with. The fortress needs to go.

Democrats need to understand and appreciate that AOC represents a brand-new constituency, one that naturally crosses ethnic and other lines, one that could actually, at long last, unify. She represents the people who want to realize the promise of a democratic (small *d*) America and who know that's being actively stifled by Trump and his corrupt, craven, overwhelmingly white male millionaire ilk. It's the people sick of reacting to Republican shenanigans and yearning to see the promise initiated. It's the people who want America to get to the business of being America. AOC talked about this, telling a story about a visit she made to D.C. with her late father, who took her to the reflecting pool and told her, "This is our Capitol. All this belongs to us." Claiming one's country as one's own, understanding that it belongs not only to you but to every other citizen, is not radical but patriotic—this land is your land, as the song goes. It's in idea that's been around the country a long time, suggested in the Constitution via "We the people," extended and humanized by the likes of Henry David Thoreau, Eugene Debs, Martin Luther King Jr., and now AOC. The country, this vast pool, should reflect all of us. "I want to live in that country," AOC has said.

Don't we all, really? In 2019 we've all been so conditioned to believe that the good life only belongs to a privileged and allegedly hardworking few; we have voluntarily taken ourselves out of the group photo; we have thrown in the towel on ever becoming a beloved community, or a Great Society, or even a society. AOC is saying there is still hope for us, that "us" is not just a musty dream of the sixties, but a necessity of the new century. It still applies. It always will. The dance is not done.

A Just Society

Tracey Ross

In the United States, one out of every three people is economically insecure. Yet "poverty" is almost entirely absent from national political discussions. Republican leaders only mention poverty when they are working to cut programs. Democratic lawmakers have retreated from a direct focus on poverty in favor of a more politically safe group: the middle class. In a recent interview, Reverend William Barber—co-chair of the Poor People's Campaign—brought this dynamic into focus, explaining, "When we even have political discussions . . . we have had the Republicans racializing poverty and Democrats running from poverty. Even the word 'poverty' has almost been removed from the political discourse. In 2016, there were 26 presidential debates. Not one was about poverty." Today, few lawmakers talk about how to support the poor—the most notable exceptions being Representatives Barbara Lee (D-CA) and

Gwen Moore (D-WI), who speak candidly about how they benefited from public assistance.

But that is changing.

With the election of Alexandria Ocasio-Cortez, people living in poverty gained another ally in Congress. Representative Ocasio-Cortez often repeats a simple yet powerful phrase: "No person should be too poor to live." As a member of the Democratic Socialists of America, she puts this belief into action by fighting for "social, economic, and racial dignity." While "socialism" and "poverty" are two words that don't seem to have a place in American politics, Ocasio-Cortez's meteoric rise is due in large part to not following the typical politician playbook.

Almost immediately following the announcement of the impeachment inquiry against President Trump, Ocasio-Cortez shared an announcement of her own through a video on Twitter. "America today is at its wealthiest point than in its entire history. And, in fact, many would argue that today the United States represents one of the richest societies in global history," she begins. "Except, in all these record profits, 40 million Americans are living in poverty. And 18.5 million Americans are living in extreme poverty, which is measured at less than $2 a day. That's why I'm so excited to introduce a suite of legislation, including five bills and one resolution, that begins to chip away at our issues of economic injustice. And we're calling it 'A Just Society.'"

The legislation would update the federal definition of poverty, advance a housing justice agenda, increase access to the social safety net for undocumented immigrants and people with criminal records, and champion worker dignity.

The "A Just Society" legislative package captures the spirit of the New Deal and the Great Society while building an anti-poverty vision inclusive of people of color, immigrants, and the modern household. Building on the momentum of the Poor People's Campaign and grassroots leaders, Ocasio-Cortez is using her platform to help advance the national conversation around eradicating poverty.

When AOC announced her legislation, I felt hopeful—despite often feeling jaded by Washington. Recalling what her championing of the Green New Deal did for the discussion on climate change, I thought, maybe we're finally going to have a real discussion about poverty. And I thought of Tianna Gaines-Turner.

Ms. Gaines-Turner is a mother, wife, advocate, and someone who has struggled with poverty for years. I was introduced to her through my work on the Poverty to Prosperity team at the Center for American Progress; she was one of our partners through Witnesses to Hunger, a research and advocacy project that centers the lived experiences of mothers and caregivers who have experienced poverty. Over the years, Gaines-Turner and her husband have struggled to get by while caring for three children who suffer from epilepsy and asthma. Despite working multiple jobs, they could not afford crucial expenses like childcare, trapping them in a cycle of poverty, including two bouts of homelessness.

When her oldest son was hospitalized, Gaines-Turner remained by his side while her husband stayed home with their twins. "We were both unable to work, so we lost money that month, and ultimately had to make a choice—do we pay the rent or do we pay the light bill? Not to mention, how do we buy food?" Such calculations were part of her everyday life. Even with food assistance, she and her husband often fed their children first and ate whatever was left over. And when they were able to secure extra hours at work, they would lose food assistance altogether.

In the midst of this hardship, Gaines-Turner used her story to advocate for herself and millions of others, taking on former House Speaker Paul Ryan, who worked tirelessly to curtail anti-poverty programs. "I am not sure at what point the American dream—of knowing that if you worked hard, you would survive—ended. But it has for my family, and for many in my communities," she stated in written testimony to Congress.

Unfortunately, Tianna's story is common. Over the last three decades, the numbers of the working poor have increased by millions. Year after year, worker power is undermined while economic gains are concentrated into fewer and fewer hands. While profits soar, wages remain stagnant, and working conditions are only getting worse. Low-wage work can take a physical toll. You can get fired for running late to your shift because your bus never showed up; or your employer can change your shift at the last minute, leaving you to struggle to figure out childcare; and wages simply aren't keeping up with the cost of living.

Women, particularly women of color, make up the majority of low-wage workers and typically earn less than $11 per hour. These women are serving food, cleaning homes and offices, and caring for children or the elderly, all while struggling to meet their own needs. Most don't have a partner's income to rely on, and many are supporting children of their own. Black and Latina women are disproportionately represented among the poor as they must also contend with past and ongoing discrimination in employment, housing, and the criminal justice system.

In 2014, Gaines-Turner was the first person living in poverty invited to speak during one of Paul Ryan's congressional hearings. After her powerful testimony, Republican congressman Todd Rokita (R-IN) asked whether she was dependent on government programs. "Yes, I consider myself to be very independent. I work just as hard as anybody in this room," Gaines-Turner replied. "I'm very independent."

"You're independent, but you're here testifying that you have to have these programs, you need these programs," Rokita responded. The exchange underscored how members of Congress are more preoccupied with demonstrating why they should cut off assistance to a Black woman, and women of color broadly, than with laying the foundation for an economy that works for everyone.

While there is an obsession over whether poor people are dependent on the government, people rarely acknowledge just how much middle- and upper-income households benefit from government spending. From the mortgage interest tax deduction to Medicare and Social Security, wealthier households enjoy a variety of government benefits. But there is no greater example of this than the spending the government does to help families build wealth. In 2017, the federal government spent $729 billion, through the tax code, on wealth-building efforts, which mainly helped already wealthy families while doing little for low- and moderate-income households. The typical benefit for a millionaire was $160,190; compare that to the typical benefit of $226 for a working family.

Our very understanding of poverty is flawed; even our poverty measure is based off what households needed to get by in the 1960s, leaving millions of economically insecure people today out of the equation. Advances in technology have altered what is necessary to fully participate in society. Climate-fueled natural disasters are part of the new normal and destroy livelihoods in a moment. And the cost of housing and other necessities has far outpaced wages.

This is why the "A Just Society" legislative package is so important. It taps into the visionary policymaking of efforts like the New Deal and the Great Society, which demonstrated that we're capable of implementing bold ideas that match the scale of the problem. And it addresses the modern realities of an increasingly diverse country.

The first bill in the package is a proposal to update the federal poverty measure to take into account new and critical expenses like childcare, Internet access, and where someone lives. Today, over 100 million people in America are economically insecure, balancing precariously on the edge of poverty. This includes the millions of people who are in jobs that do not pay family-sustaining wages, the millions of people who spend more than a third of their income on housing costs, and the millions of people struggling to come up with the money to weather an emergency. In fact, 40 percent of Americans wouldn't be able to cover the cost of a $400 emergency. Our current poverty measure doesn't capture this. This is a familiar story to Ocasio-Cortez. During her sophomore year, her father passed away, which she described as "destabilizing in every way." After college, she returned to the Bronx to help support her mother and fight the foreclosure of their home.

Amid rising inequality and persistent racial inequities, we need a better way to measure economic hardship in our nation. And we need to fight the stigma of accepting assistance. Too often, economically insecure people are met with skepticism rather than compassion. People of all income levels benefit from some sort of government support, from food assistance to tax breaks, but poor people are the only ones who face mistrust over whether or not they really deserve support. Four out of five Americans will experience at least a year of significant economic insecurity and 70 percent of us will turn to public benefits at some point in our lives.

But as history shows—from Southern states limiting the access of Black families to New Deal programs, to the "welfare reform" policies of the 1990s that punished women for having children—U.S. poverty policy often discriminates against groups deemed undeserving of support. Ocasio-Cortez's "A Just Society" legislation addresses this inequality head-on for two particularly vulnerable, yet maligned, groups: the formerly incarcerated and undocumented immigrants.

The Mercy in Re-Entry Act would allow people who were convicted of a crime and paid their debt to society to be eligible for public benefits. Currently, 30 states subject people with drug-related felony convictions to restrictions or complete bans on food or cash assistance. Women are more likely to have drug convictions than men, with women of color at greater risk due to racial disparities in the enforcement of drug laws. As a result, these women may face a lifetime ban on basic resources for themselves and their families. But when cash and food assistance are immediately available to people returning home, the likelihood of recidivism a year after release declines.

Similarly, the Embrace Act would end discrimination of federal public benefits based on one's immigration status. In the past couple years, there has been an increase in hate crimes against Latinos, which many attribute to President Trump's rhetoric against immigrants—from accusations of immigrants being gang members to claims they are draining public resources. "We have been on the defense of Trump's rhetoric—false rhetoric—for so long and I think it's about time that we challenge it," Ocasio-Cortez stated in an interview. "Immigrants contribute to our country economically. Immigrants pay taxes," she explained. "I think [the legislation] sends a message that if you contribute to our society, you should benefit from our society." This is significant as the Trump administration announced measures to deny even documented immigrants green cards, visa extensions, and immigration status changes if they received benefits. Together, these two bills challenge the notions of the undeserving and deserving poor by saying that everyone has value and should have a chance to improve their life.

One of the most comprehensive parts of A Just Society is the housing justice agenda called "The Place to Prosper Act." This bill would advance tenant protections, such as just-cause evictions and right to counsel for tenants facing eviction, crack down on predatory landlords, and pass a national rent control policy—policies grassroots leaders and tenant organizers have been championing for years. Advocates and local elected officials advancing these policies are particularly excited about this piece of the package as federal policy would accelerate their efforts and provide the resources to implement these strategies. In a recent report, PolicyLink, the Center for Popular Democracy, and the Right to the City Alliance found that if rent control was adopted across the country, 42 million households could be stabilized. Studies also show that providing legal representation to tenants facing eviction significantly decreases the likelihood of eviction.

Housing is the single largest expense people have, and its high cost is straining budgets. Today, a full-time minimum-wage worker cannot afford a one-bedroom apartment in nearly any state in the United States. And only one in four households eligible for rental assistance actually receives it due to overwhelming demand, forcing many families onto lengthy waiting lists. As a result, millions of families face housing insecurity, displacement, eviction, or homelessness.

Further, in many cities and states, landlords can legally evict tenants in favor of wealthier renters willing to pay higher prices, or even out of retaliation for requesting repairs. Evictions are all too common, particularly for Black women, who are more likely than any other group to face eviction due to factors such as having children, low wages, and landlord-tenant dynamics. Evictions also have lasting effects on employment, health, and well-being. Matthew Desmond, author of *Evicted*, describes this epidemic, explaining, "If incarceration had come to define the lives of men from impoverished Black neighborhoods, eviction was shaping the lives of women. Poor Black men were locked up. Poor Black women were locked out." The housing justice agenda is among the most thought-out parts of the package, reflecting the work of grassroots leaders and a growing housing justice movement.

The final bill in the package uses the purchasing power of the federal government as leverage for improving workers' quality of life. The Uplift Our Workers Act would create a "worker-friendly score" for federal contracts. The rating would take into account factors such as worker co-operatives, union memberships, and various pro-worker policies such as paid leave and a living wage, which are proven to increase morale, worker retention, and family incomes, among other benefits.

While this is a great strategy, legislation that outlined national worker-friendly policies—rather than just incen-tivized them—would be more powerful. The United States trails other advanced economies in job quality, which negatively impacts our ability to compete globally. While some private-sector employers voluntarily offer these ben-efits, they are often unevenly applied to their employees. Federal policy is necessary to ensure that worker dignity is restored, prosperity is shared, and our country is put on a more sustainable path.

Together, the bills that make up "A Just Society" require us to confront assumptions about what poverty is and challenge outdated narratives of the deserving and undeserving poor. The fact that AOC specifically focuses on undocumented immigrants and people with criminal records is significant, as these are two groups that are disproportionately people of color and are regularly subjected to dehumanizing rhetoric and treatment. She is not trying to legislate around the racial-ized nature of the poverty debate but to challenge it directly.

From a policy perspective, there is more to be done than what is outlined in the pages of this legislation, as I'm sure AOC would agree. From immediate goals such as raising the minimum wage to highly ambitious ideas like universal family care or a federal jobs guarantee. Lifting millions of people out of economic insecurity and closing racial gaps in employment, income, and wealth will also require working at all levels of government and across the private sector.

In the true style of movement building, Ocasio-Cortez concluded the announcement of her legislation with a call to action and an invitation to join. "In a modern, moral, and wealthy society, no person should be too poor to live. That is what a just society means to me, and I can't wait to hear what a just society means to you."

For me, a just society means your zip code does not determine your life outcomes. When it comes to escaping poverty, your neighborhood plays a significant role—influencing everything from a child's likelihood of going to college to the status of their health. In fact, your zip code plays a bigger role in your life expectancy than your genetic code. This is something I think about every day. Through leading the All-In Cities initiative at PolicyLink, I have worked with leaders in communities across the country and have seen firsthand just how persistent economic and racial inequities are. Too many low-income people, especially people of color, struggle to get by in neighborhoods characterized by poor-quality housing, environmental hazards, struggling schools, and inadequate public infrastructure. Others face displacement altogether as the effects of gentrification push them out of the communities they call home.

Today, roughly 1 in 4 Black people and 1 in 6 Latinos live in high-poverty neighborhoods, compared to just 1 in 13 white people. And it's not just about income. The average African American family making $100,000 a year lives in a more disadvantaged neighborhood than the average white family making $30,000 a year, revealing how past social policies—such as redlining and the construction of the highway system through Black neighborhoods—continue to hinder neighborhood choice. This also contributes to why Black children in middle-class families actually have downward social mobility compared to white middle-class children. While more Black people are living in distressed neighborhoods, the share of Latinos living in distressed areas rose more than other groups in the years following the recession.

In 2018, Tianna Gaines-Turner returned to Capitol Hill to highlight the negative effects of her neighborhood. Despite gaining a rewarding, full-time position at a nonprofit, she said: "I live in the Northeastern section of Philadelphia, where the poverty rate is one of the highest in the nation. When I walk out the door—I see the ravages of racism all around me. My family is practically swimming in it." She described a neighborhood with blighted buildings, where housing was in disrepair, streets were littered with trash, and the trauma of gun violence was everywhere. But she also described a community that supports one another. "It is a strong community just trying to survive and we should be celebrated." A just society is one in which Tianna

Gaines-Turner, her family, and her community can thrive without having to move.

There are proven strategies leaders can implement to ensure communities like Northeastern Philly can help rather than hinder families. Providing wraparound services for families in schools; investing in infrastructure; and the policies in AOC's housing justice agenda are all proven strategies that local leaders can champion. At the same time, federal policy can help to grow and scale local efforts, ensuring investment in all communities. For decades, the federal government invested in the strength and stability of affluent, white communities. It is time to extend that investment to all communities. That would make for a truly just society.

While it is incredibly hard to get any piece of legislation through this Congress—let alone one that would expand public benefits—for Ocasio-Cortez, it's not about passing any single piece of legislation. It's about changing the conversation in Washington. The "A Just Society" legislative package is meant to push our political discourse and challenge assumptions about poverty. If it can do that—and help poverty make its way into the 2020 election—it will have been successful. If anything, the legislation has given me this platform to share what a just society means to me, and to share Tianna Gaines-Turner's story once again. AOC's plan seems to be working already.

Latinas Are So Money

Carmen Rita Wong

In 2018, straight out of the gate, Alexandria Ocasio-Cortez, AOC, talked and tweeted about economic policy with the confidence of a white man. There she was, freshening up our screens: a young Latina with red lips and hoop earrings speaking to and challenging financial power in this country, something rarely—if ever—seen on the national political stage.

Those first few weeks, I held my breath as I watched the flood of dismissal and belittlement pour over her and her followers in waves. And I braced myself for what was still to come. I knew too well what would happen as she dared to address, *con huevos*, the world of finance, banking, and business, institutions filled with and controlled by pale males. Pale males who think of women—especially women of color—as lesser when it comes to money talk.

The vitriol coming AOC's way was all too familiar to

me. Ten years before her win, in 2008, I was the first Latina to solo-host a prime-time one-hour finance television show. It was on CNBC. I knew my stuff. I had come from an editor post at *Money* magazine and had been at *Fortune* as well. I also wrote and sold one of the first personal finance advice books by a woman of color when those things weren't done. But in spite of all this, all too often the reaction to me on the set of my show from guests—nearly always white males—was as follows:

GUEST: "Are you really Hispanic?"
GUEST: "Wow. You're smart!"

Can you imagine a white male guest on a television news show telling his white male host: "Oh, wow, you're smart!"? It would be absurd and insulting. And yet it happened all the time. Like AOC now, I was instantly assumed to be dumb, to lack authority or knowledge because I was a brown woman with a funny name who wore lipstick (and, yes, hoops!). I'll spare you the long, nasty emails I received. It was the dawn of Twitter and I was trolled daily. What did I know, right?

To cope with the slights, I made what stung into a joke. On the set of my show, I started a pantomime drinking game with my producers in the control room. While we were taping, every time a guest on set made a comment, usually during the commercial break, about my "Hispanicness" or said they were surprised that I had a brain, I would look into the camera lens, pointing through to my beloved production team watching from the control room, and say "Drink!" as we tipped back imaginary tequila shots. Some weeks, we were constantly "drunk."

The bias and hostility against women of color in the world of economics and finance are unbelievable. Here's a peek at what was handed out—in print!—at a 2019 leadership presentation to new employees of one of the largest accounting firms in the world, Ernst & Young (number of employees ≈260,000): "Women's brains absorb information like pancakes soak up syrup so it's hard for them to focus . . . Men's brains are more like waffles. They're better able to focus because the information collects in each little waffle square." The information was leaked by a (noncaveperson) attendee.

In the financial services industry (think banks, accounting, investing, sales, research, etc.), Latinas make up only 8 percent of the field overall and a dismal 5 percent of financial advisors. These numbers are among the worst of all the industries in the United States, but understandable. Why would any woman anywhere want to work in an industry that has proven unwelcoming, especially if there are other choices? The backward thinking and the doors closed to women can lead to a lot of trouble and pain for those brave enough to take on this world. And those who research and teach "money" to the finance industry fare no better. The American Economic Association reported in 2019 that 58 percent of Latinas have experienced racism and/or gender discrimination at work in the field of economics.

I'm surprised the number is not higher considering how recent the history of women in the field is. In 1967, Muriel "Mickie" Siebert was the first woman to be approved to buy a seat on the New York Stock Exchange. It would take ten years for another woman to join her. At present, only 85 of the over 1,300 seats on the NYSE belong to women. The first woman to be named president of the NYSE in its 227-year history, Stacey Cunningham (elected 2018), said: "We still struggle to get a lot of women into finance."

Before Siebert passed away, I was lucky enough to host a fundraiser where this legend was the keynote speaker. Siebert spoke of how when she got her seat, there wasn't even a women's bathroom in the tens of thousands of square feet and multiple floors of the NYSE. She told us, "I had to go outside!" She had to walk to another building to find a women's bathroom, at a time when leaving your trading desk could cost you money.

The odds were and are stacked against us. So, we work harder, push through, deal with catcalls and butt grabs, plantain and glass ceilings 20 miles thick, and the assumption that we don't know what we're talking about. But we do. And that matters. After all, AOC was smart enough to have an asteroid named after her by MIT (M-I-freakin'-T, *mi gente!*), and yet, headlines like "Alexandria Ocasio-Cortez Is an Economic Illiterate" have been showing up since before she was sworn into office.

Is she always right? No one is. But the power she has is twofold: (1) She has the confidence of conviction. She understands that money and economic policies shape our lives in this country, particularly the lives of people of color. (2) Her knowledge of the system is the fuel she uses to push ahead through the pile-on of dudes dismissing her at every turn. As she said in 2019, "We are at our richest point that we've ever been, but we've also been our most unequal. It's something that we have to talk about."

I didn't live in the world of money for nearly 20 years because I'm an accountant. I covered the financial world because, just like AOC, I know it runs the world. And as soon as I realized that it's a system unfair to our people, my fire was lit. But this driving force was not something I could share directly with my all-white colleagues at *Money* magazine in the late nineties. That's the reason I pushed hard to move forward and take on more, because I felt the weight of all the people who didn't have the advantage of growing up with money or knowing how to manage money. And I knew that there was no reason why we, Latinx or anyone else, shouldn't be a member of this very special club.

AOC has spoken often and eloquently about her family's financial struggles. This direct experience of financial inequality combined with a college degree in international relations and economics means that she is not intimidated by the world of money.

It took a white man and a financial crisis for me to learn about money. My mother's second husband, my Italian

American stepfather, Charlie, was a graduate student of economics at Columbia University when they met. His white-collar career moved us into a different financial reality. I wasn't really into sports, so to bond with this new, more fancy father, I got curious about his interest in finance, which was a big part of his daily routine. I would ask him about the lists of stocks he'd pore over daily, his head buried in the newspaper (the tiny lines of daily stock prices looked like powerful hieroglyphics to me), or I'd watch financial news shows with him, asking questions mostly to build a relationship. There were piles of *Money* and *Fortune* magazines in the house. And when I was 12, he took me to the bank to open my first savings account (with a printed ledger!). It all stuck.

And then the good fortune ended. And I saw how the stock market can affect us—how we can lose our homes— even if we don't own any stock at all. When Black Monday hit the stock market in October 1987, plunging the country into a recession, our household turned from giving to receiving church aid; our breadwinning dad lost his job that same day and didn't find work again for years.

So when I showed up at the offices in the Time-Life Building in Rockefeller Center in my early twenties and the only opening was at *Money* magazine, I said, "Sure. I know that stuff." And what I found out on the job (besides the incredible resistance to anyone of color having any role beyond an assistant or receptionist in this field) was that some white folks had grown up talking about money at a sophisticated level. It was normal—as it had been in my house with a white stepdad. It was like a club, a club with an inordinate amount of power. What if we all grew up like this? I thought. What if this information was easily accessed by everyone?

This was a time before you could google, before my money advice columns (or any money articles) appeared in women's and men's general interest magazines or on morning TV shows or anywhere beyond the finance world or the business section. A small group of people controlled all the financial information, education, policy, and regulation for the whole nation. *Imagínate.*

To not know how money and the system work is to fall prey to them. The financial system all too often exploits our lack of knowledge. After the Great Recession of 2008, Wells Fargo was fined for creating and pushing bad and overly expensive loans for people of color. State Street Bank paid fines for underpaying women and minorities. This, by the way, was the bank that funded the "Fearless Girl" statue in front of the New York Stock Exchange. And, of course, we all should know about the pay gap: Latinas earn only 54 cents for every dollar a white man earns.

And yet, amazingly, Ocasio-Cortez was appointed to the House Financial Services Committee, chaired by the indomitable 81-year-old, 15-term representative Maxine Waters (D-CA) of the famous public declaration "I'm reclaiming my time!"

This committee is a big deal. In terms of the finance

world, it is *the* deal. This committee oversees all banking, lending, and finance in this country. It oversees the U.S. Treasury, the Federal Reserve, and the U.S. Securities and Exchange Commission (the "cops" of the finance industry), as well as the FDIC and the Consumer Financial Protection Bureau. Take a moment to appreciate that the all-white, all-male CEOs (no women) of all the big banks are being overseen by a committee led by an African American legend of a woman, Ms. Waters, joined by a Puerto Rican millennial, speaking reality to power through the bullhorn of millions upon millions of social media followers and a very attentive press. AOC is savvy. She knows the power and symbolism of her presence in this arena, and she uses it to great effect.

In a 2019 hearing of the House Financial Services Committee on the burden of student debt, AOC paid her student loan bill live during the hearing: "I literally made a student loan payment while I was sitting here at this chair, and I looked at my balance, and it was $20,237.16. I just made a payment that took me down to $19,000 so I feel really accomplished right now." The national student loan debt is over $1.5 trillion, and nearly one-third of her fellow members of Congress carry student loan balances as well. AOC brings no shame in talking about her money, especially if it helps to normalize the burden of debt. She was paying her bill in public and on the record, making the point that it is time to challenge and change the status quo.

She brings that same effectiveness to challenging the

Masters of the Universe. Mark Zuckerberg, the billionaire founder of Facebook, has been trying to create a financial arm of Facebook, to create a type of cryptocurrency like Bitcoin. This is from a site that has arguably changed world politics—this country's in particular—forever with its lack of oversight during the 2016 election. This same Zuckerberg wants to manage our money?

Here's AOC, age 30, grilling a visibly frazzled robot, a titan of Silicon Valley, age 35, at a hearing of the House Financial Services Committee regarding the spread of disinformation Facebook allows and a draft bill, the Keep Big Tech Out of Finance Act:

AOC: Do you see a potential problem here with a complete lack of fact-checking on political advertisements?

ZUCKERBERG: Well, Congresswoman, I think lying is bad. And I think if you were to run an ad that had a lie that would be bad. That's different from it being—from—in our position, the right thing to do to prevent your constituents or people in an election from seeing that you had lied.

AOC: So, we can—so, you won't take down lies, or you will take down lies? I think this is just a pretty simple yes or no.

ZUCKERBERG: Congresswoman, in—

AOC: I'm not talking about spin. I'm talking about actual disinformation.

ZUCKERBERG: Yes. In most cases, in a democracy—

AOC: Okay.

ZUCKERBERG: I believe that people should be able to see for themselves what politicians, that they may or may not vote for, are saying—

AOC: So you won't take them down?

Zuckerberg twisted himself into knots working to evade Ocasio-Cortez's direct questions. (Her delivery on that "simple yes or no" may remind many of us of our Latina mothers—or ourselves.)

But this "top C-Span hit" was not AOC's first triumph of a congressional hearing. Not even a year into her post, there she was, dressed in two layers of a saturated Yves Klein blue, the youngest elected member of the House, leaning with authority into the mic, ready for her allotted five minutes. She was challenging the CEO of one of the largest banks in the world. In the spring of 2019, AOC forced JPMorgan Chase's CEO, Jamie Dimon, to speak to the way in which laws and consequences tend to apply to the poor, rather than the heavily banked (a.k.a. rich), in a hearing of the finance committee:

AOC: Okay, in my district, I represent Rikers Island. I represent kids that go to jail for jumping a turnstile because they can't afford a MetroCard. Do you think that more folks should have gone to jail for their role in a financial crisis that led to 7.8 million foreclosures?

JAMIE DIMON: I don't think people should go to jail for jumping the subway.

Dimon's response is deflective and condescending. In that question, and his answer, the world could see America's dirty laundry. Money gives you power. Power to avoid punishment. And a lack of money and the wrong skin tone primes you for a system with a narrow chance of escape.

This was a far cry from when, in the midst of the Great Recession, I interviewed the head of the Securities and Exchange Commission (SEC), pressing him for explanations as to why the government agency in charge of policing the finance industry let the banks create reckless products that led to the loss of homes and assets for millions of Americans. My bosses weren't happy with my line of questioning—hello, doing my job—and they particularly were not happy with the confidence in my voice and the lack of a smile. How dare I? Only ten years ago, before AOC, we (women, especially brown women) weren't allowed to be publicly angry and press against power on air. Leave that to the guys.

So by the time AOC tackled an even bigger beast—the president—with the same smoking gun that took down Al Capone—taxes—I was practically shaking pom-poms with joy. Using the serious game of follow the money, she questioned Trump's former attorney, Michael Cohen, about his boss deflating the value of his golf club in Jupiter, Florida, to purposely lower his tax bill (a.k.a. fraud):

AOC: To your knowledge, was the president interested in lowering his local real estate tax bills?

COHEN: Yes.

AOC may make it farther than any Latina in our elected government before her, and I believe it will be due to this particular fire for economic justice and her knowledge of the financial services industry.

Because, after all, what drives AOC is a set of values. Values that, were they not yet clear to folks, she stated succinctly in a 2019 hearing on the disastrous dealings of private equity firms that bought up companies (like Toys"R"Us) only to lay off thousands of employees while pocketing millions for themselves: "I wasn't sent here to safeguard and protect profit. I was sent here to safeguard and protect people."

This isn't about agreeing with her stances on all these issues. I know I don't. This is about understanding how revolutionary it is to have someone who looks like us, who shares our history and our expansive underrepresented culture, speaking to power. And money—boring, scary money—is key to leveling the playing field. AOC knows that. Now millions more of us are getting to know and see that, too.

Like my mother, who passed away from cancer, leaving behind nothing but bills. Or my brother, who now has cancer too and is unable to work. Even with insurance coverage, he's accumulating piles of bills to sort and pay, stressful work in addition to his job of staying alive for his family and maybe, just maybe, making it down the stairs for dinner.

My strongest hope is that many more of us, like AOC, turn the halls of government and finance less pale and less male. May we make the changes that make this nation more fair and shift the burden from resting so heavily on us and our families. I hope to be raising my pom-poms for more rebel-rousing Latinas. Maybe it will be you.

AOC the Influencer

Mariana Atencio

87,300,000.

That is the number of results a simple Google search of Alexandria Ocasio-Cortez, aka AOC, will get you less than one year after she assumed office as the representative for New York's 14th congressional district.

In 2018, she was ranked the fifth-most-googled politician in the United States. In 2019 she was the most talked-about politician on Tinder. She graced the cover of *Time* magazine as one of its most influential people of 2019 before even hitting the 100-day mark in Congress. Her relevance goes beyond the Hill, making her a topic of conversation at dinner dates and in almost any other environment in the country.

Alexandria Ocasio-Cortez has been idolized, criticized, and scrutinized to the point of having to respond to the conservative outlet *Washington Times* for a "high-dollar hairdo," after paying $300 for a haircut, lowlights, and tip.

A pretty reasonable price for that service if you ask any professional woman with shoulder-length hair living in an expensive city such as Washington, D.C.

Everything she says or does has the potential to ignite controversy in a matter of minutes, especially when it concerns President Donald Trump. The two have been at odds many times. In the summer of 2019, the president caused nationwide outrage when he tweeted that AOC, and her "squad" of progressive congresswomen of color, should "go back and help fix the totally broken and crime infested places from which they came."

AOC shot back: "Mr. President, the country I come from and the country we all swear to, is the United States." The thread racked up thousands of comments from both sides of the political aisle.

Despite having told *HuffPost* that "sometimes I just want to be a human being," AOC understands that all the attention gives her power, too. She has reconciled her mixed feelings on losing her privacy by saying: "I can't afford to be hidden away. In order for me to do my job, I need to be connected to people."

I first realized the reach of that connection on January 19, 2019. It was the third anniversary of the Women's March. Hundreds of thousands of women, of all ages and backgrounds, took to the streets in cities across the United States to rally for their rights. They stood side by side— white, black, Asian, Latino, LGBTQ+, immigrant—in a sea of unity.

The chants and messages that day were filled with enough determination to change the world.

"In 2018 we made gains. In 2019 we make demands," one banner read defiantly. There was a sense of empowerment and purpose in the streets, so powerful you could feel it in your bones.

I was reporting for MSNBC's *AM Joy* from the march in New York City, as a crowd gathered outside the Trump International Hotel and Tower. I was on live TV when a young woman wearing gold hoops and red lipstick walked behind me. It was none other than Alexandria Ocasio-Cortez. She paused and smiled, even giving a wink, directly at the camera. *Sí*, she literally photobombed me!

"When @AOC does the Beyoncé photobomb on you @ MSNBC," I tweeted.

The moment went viral, as the congresswoman reacted and retweeted me by saying: "We meme IRL [in real life] too." The tweet has been liked almost 8,000 times.

As a millennial journalist, I understand the impact that social media has for a public figure. I have posted about the news I cover and its implications for nearly a decade. I have met people from all walks of life and have brought their stories to America's living rooms. From reporting on student-led protests in the nation's capital to walking with migrant asylum seekers at the southern border to speaking to those affected by natural disasters in Puerto Rico, the Bahamas, and the Florida panhandle, to running up and down the corridors of Congress . . . you could say I chase hurricanes and politicians for a living.

When I later asked @AOC, as she's known in the Twitterverse, what the historic Women's March meant to her personally, she was beaming with the same enthusiasm as the other women at the march. "We are still taking up presence and we're going to push for the agenda that we elected so many people to advance," she said.

Then and there everything clicked for me. At just 30 years old, Alexandria Ocasio-Cortez is elevating the agenda on social media and rewriting the traditional rules of governance with every post. Her impact makes it clear that representation matters and that the present is female. She is not waiting for anybody to fix what she believes to be wrong with the system. She is doing it herself, and that's a powerful message at a time when lots of politicians just keep pandering to women and minority issues.

In a political climate where Latinos are under attack, she's the second-most-talked-about politician in America, behind only President Donald Trump. Today, Ocasio-Cortez boasts nearly 11 million followers across Twitter, Instagram, and Facebook.

The first politician to truly leverage the grassroots power of social media was Barack Obama during the 2008 presidential election. Fast-forward to 2019, and nearly every politician in Washington has a social media handle, from President Trump dictating foreign policy using 280 characters on Twitter, to Senator Elizabeth Warren announcing she is running for president while having a beer on Instagram.

What makes someone a social media influencer in a digital world where anybody can achieve instant recognition with a stroke of luck? With the exception of the inevitable haters and trolls, most people follow influencers for aspirational, positive, reliable, and relatable content.

Influencers share their trajectory, successes, and even disappointments with their audiences. Authenticity is key to building trust. From the very beginnings of her campaign, Ocasio-Cortez's voice was not only real for her supporters, it was also relatable.

Thousands tune in regularly to watch her talk politics on IGTV or Instagram Live while she is cooking dinner or assembling IKEA furniture and sipping wine. During these sessions, she has touched on climate change, Puerto Rico, and President Trump's tax returns. She has also admitted that since becoming a congresswoman, she hasn't had time to furnish her apartment and for a while she was sleeping on a mattress on the floor. What could be more relatable?

The millennial generation has often been criticized for "hashtag activism" because some feel that they post about critical issues—from racism and police brutality to sexual assault and inequality—without actually having skin in the game. President Obama made headlines when he said that today's callout culture is "not activism."

However, AOC, who was an activist before running for office, makes sure that her social media goes together with actual civic participation. Unlike her older colleagues, the @AOC phenomenon emerged with social media. She's influenced lawmaking, called out critics, and built a lasting brand known not just domestically but around the world.

The Bronx native represents her *gente* by being unapologetically Latina. In a room full of members who have held their congressional seats for as long as most millennials and Gen Zers have been alive, she is creating a path for a new generation of lawmakers.

She uses her social platforms to stop us in our tracks as we scroll through our feeds, forcing us to listen to the voices of those who are underrepresented and marginalized.

Like many Americans, I first learned about Alexandria Ocasio-Cortez through her viral campaign ad on Twitter in the spring of 2018. In one scene, she gets ready for a day of work, changing into her professional heels before jumping onto the New York City subway and heading into Manhattan.

One woman reacted to the video: "My daughter saw one of your posters and asked me *¿Quién es esa señora?* I told her your story, she said: *Mamá* she is like me! She cut your picture and has it in her desk. #ThanksForRunning #WishYouTheBest."

"Can you send me a *fotito* {photo} of her desk? I want to carry it with me," @AOC tweeted back.

A couple of days later, the woman sent Ocasio-Cortez the photo she asked for. Then, after a few months, the same voter followed up, this time with a photo of her entire family canvassing for AOC's campaign. "We count on you be-cause we see you as #OneOfUs," she captioned the image.

A bond was formed. Not just with this woman, but with thousands of others who felt ignored and distanced from the members of Congress elected to represent them.

After her historic primary win, Ocasio-Cortez responded to critics who downplayed the moment by posting her "campaign shoes," the ones she wore to knock on doors "until rainwater came through my soles." She urged crit-ics claiming her win was purely "demographic" to "respect the hustle."

It worked. When it comes to her meteoric rise, the num-bers, in fact, say it all. According to the Federal Election Commission, the congresswoman raised a total of $2 mil-lion during her 2018 election campaign. Ocasio-Cortez has the highest rate of small-dollar funding among current U.S. House members, and over 60 percent of those funds came directly from individual contributions of less than $200. This kind of grassroots support from the very beginning showed that working-class New Yorkers were by her side.

Her competition is taking notice, especially at a time in our country's history when younger voter turnout is quickly increasing. Over the last five years, we have seen a 20 percent increase in 18- to 29-year-olds voting. More high-profile politicians are shifting their strategies to in-corporate youth.

When AOC first stepped into Congress to represent more than 700,000 people across parts of the Bronx and

Queens, she set the tone for what her next two years would look like, all through a series of tweets that went viral. In one of the first, she used a play on Bronx superstar Jennifer Lopez's lyrics to caption a photo of the plaque outside her office with her name, title, and state engraved on it: "Don't be fooled by the plaques that we got, I'm still / I'm still Alex from the Bronx." It was a vivid reminder to stay humble and never forget her roots.

A Pew Research Center survey found that most Americans believe social media is helpful when it comes to two things: getting elected officials to pay attention and launching social movements to enact sustainable political change.

As a journalist, I check most politicians' latest posts to learn more about them and their agendas. Whether it's an article they share or a photo of them at work, all of it offers insight into their persona, priorities, the laws they are working to pass, and their interactions with constituents.

Posts portraying authenticity and consideration are the ones that catch most people's attention and hearts. The congresswoman posted a photo on her Instagram looking down at her basket full of groceries. @AOC shared that while she is working to pay off her student loans, she is grateful for every little grain of rice and the beans on her plate. She expressed her commitment to work for everyone to have a basket full of groceries just like hers.

During an interview on *The Late Show with Stephen Colbert*, Ocasio-Cortez revealed that she was asked to teach other members of Congress what it takes to be a social media–savvy politician. She shared with them the dos and don'ts of Twitter, as well as her personal strategies for connecting with people through the web.

Her advice included:

"Be authentic, be yourself and don't try to be anyone that you're not."

"Don't post a meme if you don't know what a meme is."

"Don't talk like the Founding Fathers on Twitter."

This wasn't simply a Social Media 101 lesson. It illustrated that the next generation had arrived, and they had a lot to teach those in power. It was a breath of fresh air in a space where politicians don't seem as clever and authentic as AOC. That's the difference. She doesn't simplify, she cuts to the chase.

Ocasio-Cortez's ability to communicate with voters was, and still is, her winning card. She takes time to explain, in great detail, whatever her followers want to talk about.

In one of her Instagram posts she boldly said aloud what many unpaid Washington interns have whispered for years: "Experience doesn't pay the bills." The five-second clip #PayOurInterns received over two million views and sparked a heated debate. It's what Ocasio-Cortez does best: put a finger on the spot and make people face uncomfortable issues.

Granted, everyone has the right to disagree, as her opponents do, often viciously. But, as a true Bronx girl, she is quick to fight back.

On the eve of her swearing-in ceremony, a supposedly "scandalous" video of a younger Ocasio-Cortez was leaked. She was seen dancing and twirling to Phoenix's "Lisztomania" with fellow students on a rooftop at her alma mater, Boston University.

Within hours, the video was circulating all over the country. Her supporters loved it—sparking a series of memes online. But her opponents quickly criticized it, claiming it discredited her leadership.

Ocasio-Cortez's witty comeback nearly broke the internet. She responded to the "accusations" by posting a video of herself dancing in front of her new office. With Edwin Starr's "War" lyrics "What is it good for / Absolutely nothing" playing in the background, she captioned it: "I hear the GOP thinks women dancing are scandalous. Wait till they find out Congresswomen dance too!"

It racked up more than 21 million views in less than five hours, becoming Ocasio-Cortez's most retweeted post.

Civil rights activist Shaun King said the university video "proves that she's basically been cool forever."

Her passion is contagious and prompts people to act and react. We saw this play out when Amazon announced it would open the company's second headquarters in Long Island City, Queens.

Ocasio-Cortez tweeted: "1 in 10 of Amazon's Ohio employees were on food stamps after the company opened fulfillment centers in the state." Encouraged by her support, among other things, local opposition and grassroots activists took to the streets and flooded Amazon stores to rally against the company's plans.

The public pressure eventually forced Amazon to cancel its HQ2 in New York.

The company stated in a blog post that "a state member and local politicians have made it clear that they oppose our presence and will not work with us."

Congresswoman Ocasio-Cortez has made it a priority, too, to focus on the engagement of Americans in U.S. politics. The game plan of an efficient lawmaker is not just thinking about the present but also looking toward the future. It is impossible to predict how long it will take for a bill to be passed in Congress. That's why it's so fundamental for politicians to define the agenda for the next generations.

With a winning mix of fact-checking, witty comebacks, relatable anecdotes, and emojis, this Latina politician found her voice on social media and shared it with the world.

So, here is my #TopTen list of tweets by @AOC that will probably make it into history books or digital courses in the near future.

1. After Amazon pulled out of building a fulfillment center in NYC, then later announced they would be opening offices in Manhattan, she posed in a waiting room: "Me waiting on the haters to apologize after we were proven right on Amazon and saved the public billions."

2. When Uber designated separate bathrooms for drivers and white-collar workers: "Siri, show me what classism looks like."

3. When Fox News used graphics that read "GET USED TO ME SLAYING," she wrote, "Thank you Fox News for making all the campaign graphics I never knew I needed."

4. When critics insisted she agree to debate Ben Shapiro: "Just like catcalling, I don't owe a response to unsolicited requests from men with bad intentions. And also like catcalling, for some reason they feel entitled to one."

5. When the Democrats tweeted an advertisement of a Beyoncé wallpaper: "Someone didn't go to my Twitter class."

6. When she faced criticism for her congressional attire, she wrote, "If I walked into Congress wearing a sack, they would laugh & take a picture of my backside. If I walk in with my best sale-rack clothes, they laugh & take a picture of my backside. Dark hates light—that's why you tune it out. Shine bright & keep it pushing."

7. When critics tweeted a photo of the house she grew up in and got her alma mater wrong, she responded, "Hey John,
   1. I didn't go to Brown or the Ivy League. I went to BU. Try Google.

2. It is nice. Growing up, it was a good town for working people. My mom scrubbed toilets so I could live here & I grew up seeing how the zip code one is born in determines much of their opportunity."

8. When she schooled Fox News on being Latina: "If by 'the Latina thing,' she means I actually do the work instead of just talk about it, then yeah, I'm doing 'the Latina thing.' Unless of course she's talking about being multilingual, which we know isn't a 'Latina thing.' It's a '21st century' thing."

9. When she complained about the price of a croissant to demand value for human labor: "Croissants at LaGuardia are going for SEVEN DOLLARS A PIECE. Yet some people think getting a whole hour of personal, dedicated human labor for $15 is too expensive??"

10. When she awarded a critic who told her to stop calling members of Congress "congressmembers" an emoji trophy: "Here is your Twitter Prescriptivism Prize 🏆 while you're at it, try capitalizing my name next time."

Since we did pay attention to her Twitter class, there's just one more thing to say: like @AOC, you have the tools to make a difference: "Activism disrupts the present to change the future."

Now go tweet, share, repost, and like it!

What AOC and I Learned at Standing Rock

Wendy Carrillo

Are activists born or made? I can trace my own path to supporting the Green New Deal all the way back to a childhood beach day.

I must have been around ten years old when I first volunteered for a beach cleanup. I couldn't tell you the name of the organization that put the event on or how I even ended up on a bus from East Los Angeles to Cabrillo Beach State Park. Perhaps the trip was sponsored by Heal the Bay and the Boys and Girls Club from my neighborhood. I don't remember, but I still very clearly recall the light blue bags we were given and the feeling of immense sadness and anger that I experienced picking up discarded cigarettes, empty plastic bags of chips, and those awful plastic six-ring soda holders popular back in the eighties and early nineties.

On that trip I learned to cut those soda plastic rings into pieces so that they wouldn't get tangled on the neck or body of a sea turtle, potentially killing it or stunting its growth. The pictures they showed our group were pretty explicit. Freshly vigilant, I headed home with my new-found knowledge. I took my environmentalist role very seriously, showing my little sister and my parents everything I had learned. I went on and on, arms flailing, eyes wide with excitement, gushing, sharing tales about marine life, all the while translating everything into Spanish! *Las tortugas! Hay que proteger las tortugas!*

A year or so later, I was on the deck of a ship departing from the Long Beach pier to Catalina Island for environmental science camp. I had sold endless boxes of chocolates so I could afford the trip. I was one of the top sellers in my school and it would be my first time on a ship! I was very excited. I was embarking on three glorious days away from my parents to learn about ecosystems, birds, sea lions, and coral reefs. I made my way to the very front of the ferry, the water splashing around the sides and occasionally onto the few of us kids courageous enough to lean over the rail just a bit.

Then I saw them.

A group of beautiful dolphins appeared below, jumping up from the ocean waves alongside our ship. Squeaking and giggling, they were magical and playful. They made my heart so happy. I felt like a tiny speck in a universe so large and full of wonders that I had yet to discover. Those three days at that camp changed my young life. I became conscious of my impact, my consumption, my trash, and my role in being a good steward of our shared blue planet. Who was I in this vast big world? What role would I play? How could I save the turtles?

Was I the sixth planeteer in Captain Planet's world? Damn right, I was!

Looking back, I was just a little girl from East LA with working-class immigrant parents. Our means were modest but their moral values grounded me; they made me believe I could make a difference. Most importantly, my parents encouraged me. Nothing was ever too crazy or weird for them; they always went along with the ideas I brought home.

Some 25 years later, I was a journalist covering the #NoDAPL protests at Standing Rock Sioux Reservation in North Dakota. The protesters were fighting the construction of a proposed oil pipeline by the company Energy Transfer that Sioux tribe members said would endanger the reservation's primary water source and damage sacred sites. I arrived at Standing Rock in October 2016. I was supposed to be there for two weeks and ended up staying over two months. I documented the growing number of water protectors there, from ten people to thousands. Face-offs with law enforcement had become the norm and had grown increasingly hostile.

The Oceti Sakowin camp was booming with people from all walks of life answering a call to protect the sacred, to protect tribal sovereignty and the Missouri River, which provides clean water not only to the Standing Rock Sioux tribe but to 11 million Americans as well.

As a journalist, I had been covering protest culture around the world and the rise of citizen social media reporting. I had reported on riots from Baltimore to Ferguson as the United States saw an increase in cell phone documentation of police shootings against unarmed civilians.

On the night of November 21, 2016, I was handed a blue backpack filled with milk of magnesia, packets of hand warmers, and hypothermia wraps to help aid the water protectors who were engaged in a confrontation with law enforcement at a bridge that connected the camp to the pipeline project. I made my way to the front of the group, close to the barricade, my official Standing Rock press pass displayed outside my jacket. It was −20°F.

What I witnessed and experienced that night changed the course of my life. I saw people being hosed with water cannons—an international human rights violation given the frigid conditions. I saw people's clothes instantly freeze on their bodies. I saw other people rush to their aid, help them strip off their wet clothes, and provide them with warm clothing.

Then, suddenly, canisters were flying over my head.

The police were using tear gas. Everything slowed down. Something exploded next to me. A flash grenade. I saw the smoke rise. I saw a young man drop to the ground and pick up a red glowing flare that had been thrown to our side by law enforcement. He threw it right back. The red light cast an eerie glow in the night sky.

It was at that moment I remembered a game my sister and I used to play when we were little girls. We would pretend we were the little mermaid becoming human and we would hold our breath every time our parents drove through a tunnel. That's what I thought of at that moment. *Hold your breath, you're the little mermaid, swim to the surface. Stay calm.*

I pulled the turtleneck I was wearing over my nose and mouth and closed my eyes. I started to retrace my steps, unable to see, hoping I was heading toward safety.

Around me, I heard people throw up. I heard people cry out in pain. Someone fell, and I heard a young man yell: "Come on, Grandpa! We have to get out of here!"

The elders had been in a circle drumming, singing traditional Lakota songs. They, too, were teargassed. No one was spared.

I was coughing. My eyes hurt, my lungs felt like they were on fire. Someone offered me water. I poured milk of magnesia on a young girl's eyes for the second time that evening. She was crying.

It was like a war zone . . . on tribal land.

I made it back to my tent that night, and woke up the following morning feeling like a different person. I had lost all fear. I had made it through the night relatively unharmed. Some weren't as lucky and had to be taken to nearby hospitals for their injuries. A young woman almost lost her arm due to an explosion, another nearly lost her eye after being hit in the face with a rubber bullet. They both have had multiple surgeries.

President Barack Obama had previously ordered the U.S. Army Corps of Engineers to halt the pipeline, but under President Donald Trump, the project eventually moved forward and was completed. TransCanada and Energy Transfer had won.

What was it all for?

For me, that question was answered in late 2016, when a special congressional election was called to fill the newly vacated seat for the 34th congressional district—that is, my community, right where I grew up and lived. In his farewell speech to the nation, President Obama said, "If you're disappointed by your elected officials, grab a clipboard, get some signatures and run for office yourself." So I did. I ran for Congress. It was the first election following the 2016 presidential election, and it earned me national media attention and an opportunity to speak at the first Women's March in Washington, D.C.

As Standing Rock changed the course of my life, it also inspired AOC. Amid the over 10,000 people who were camped out, our paths did not cross, but we were both changed, and we were both called to service for a purpose bigger than ourselves. It is clear to me now: the power of protest is real. The power of impact, of seeing firsthand people help strangers and build community in the fight for a greater good, of seeing what can and should be versus what is, is powerful, it's life altering.

While I did not win my congressional seat, my attempt set the stage for something different. At the time, #persist was trending. I made the decision to run again, this time for a newly vacated State Assembly seat, two special elections back-to-back. The short story: I launched my congressional campaign on December 5, 2016, and won my Assembly seat on December 5, 2017, exactly one year later. I now represent the 500,000 residents of Assembly district 51 and the 40 million people who call California home.

Six months later, AOC went on to win her historic congressional election against a ten-term incumbent Democrat during the midterm elections of June 2018.

And so here we are—both fighting for the ideals of the Green New Deal. At its core it's about equity, good union jobs, and clean energy.

In California, reducing greenhouse gas emissions is already a priority. One of the most sweeping pieces of legislation, AB 32, "The Global Warming Solutions Act of 2006," authored by Assembly speaker Fabian Nuñez and Assembly member Fran Pavley, was signed into law by Governor Arnold Schwarzenegger and mandates that the state develop regulations to reduce California's greenhouse gas emissions (GHG) to 1990 levels by 2020. In 2016, AB 32 was strengthened with SB 32 by then-senator Pavley; SB 32 mandates that GHG emissions be 40 percent below 1990 levels by 2030, and was signed into law by Governor Jerry

Brown. Additionally, SB 100, authored by State Senate president pro tempore Kevin de León and of which I am a proud co-author, sets a goal of 100 percent fossil fuel–free electricity by 2045. To some, this goal may sound as ambitious as the Green New Deal, but in California, the work is being done.

The State Building and Construction Trades Council of California employs 450,000 people in 180 local unions and 22 regional building trades councils and has invested resources in good climate policy, with a commitment to building a low-carbon economy, advocating for union jobs, and creating local hire and project labor agreements (PLAs). The investment in California's Renewables Portfolio Standard (RPS) has led to apprenticeship programs and PLAs for the state's renewable-energy solar farms in places like the San Joaquin Valley, one of the poorest regions in the state.

According to the study "California's San Joaquin Valley: A Region and Its Children Under Stress," the San Joaquin Valley in Central California, while rich in oil production, land development, and agriculture, is also home to the state's most vulnerable communities of immigrants and non-citizens, who live in poverty and lack basic necessities like clean drinking water, healthy food, and clean air.

This example is one of many in which economic justice, family-sustaining jobs, renewable energy, and the future of California meet; all are pillars of the Green New Deal.

While California invests $1.5 billion per year in incentives for energy-efficient retrofits, part of our job in the legislature will be to ensure those public dollars are invested with good contractors, PLAs, and apprenticeship programs that provide a just transition of work from traditional to renewable energy opportunities.

From projects like building a new high-speed rail and light rail to creating more electric vehicle charging stations to retrofitting buildings to building affordable housing around transit corridors, there are opportunities at every turn.

While the Green New Deal may seem new, it's not. In fact, similar legislation was first introduced in the American Recovery and Reinvestment Act of 2009, otherwise known as the stimulus, by President Obama. Hidden in plain sight in the $800 billion package was $90 billion earmarked for renewable energy, clean electricity, green jobs, and more.

It's now ten years later, and while California has put in the time and effort to bring about a cleaner, more prosperous world, this moment in our history mandates that we act faster.

Climate scientists are in agreement. In the 2019 report "World Scientists' Warning of a Climate Emergency," 11,258 scientists from 153 countries and with various areas of expertise put it plainly that our planet "clearly and unequivocally faces a climate emergency."

The role of government is to protect and serve the people, to protect and serve the 12-year-old girl who at this moment is just learning about sea turtles and beach cleanups. Who deserves a fighting chance to have clean water, clean air, and a healthy planet. It is up to us to deliver that. It is up to us to make the impossible possible and, above all else, to inspire a nation to do what is right, what is just, and what is necessary. This is why AOC's leadership on the national stage is critical, why her pushing of the limits matters. Courageous, transformational leadership is what moves a nation and a world forward. Our survival depends on it.

The Democratic Socialism of AOC

Nathan J. Robinson

Alexandria Ocasio-Cortez's status as the youngest woman ever elected to Congress would be noteworthy even if she wasn't so ideologically distinct from other legislators. Anyone who has seen AOC speak at a live event understands that she has formidable energy and rhetorical talent.

But AOC is not just a dynamic young Democrat who pulled off a historic upset. She's also an unabashed democratic socialist who came to office under the banner of the Democratic Socialists of America. She is part of an ascendant movement that challenges Washington orthodoxy and offers a kind of proud working-class left politics that hasn't been seen in Congress for many years. She has made it clear that she is in Congress to create very specific kinds of social change. So unless we understand what democratic socialism means, we can't fully appreciate what AOC stands for or what she is trying to do.

Public opinion on the word "socialism" has been softening rapidly over the last few years, in part thanks to the surprisingly successful primary run of Bernie Sanders in 2016 (a campaign on which AOC worked as an organizer). The majority of young people today are more sympathetic to socialism than capitalism, and 70 percent say they would vote for a socialist.[1] This turn is remarkable: for many years, the "socialist" label was seen as political suicide. To run as a socialist was to guarantee electoral oblivion; even Green Party members stayed away from the term. One of the only elected officials in the country who wore it proudly was Bernie Sanders of Vermont, who had a reputation as a crankish outsider.

There have been socialists in Congress before, though not many. Victor Berger of Wisconsin, a co-founder of the Socialist Party of America, was a moderate reformer who served several successful terms in the 1920s (after initially being denied the right to take his seat) and helped push for old-age insurance programs. East Harlem elected Vito Marcantonio to the House in 1939. A former member of the Republican Party, he ultimately joined the leftist American Labor Party and might have been the furthest-left member in the history of Congress. Ron Dellums, the first African American elected to Congress from Northern California, was the most visible congressional socialist of the postwar era and fought the Reagan administration over South African apartheid.[2] Despite the proud work of these individuals, they remained gadflies, and there have never been enough socialists in Congress to fill a station wagon.

This is not to say that American socialism has been insignificant. In fact, in its heyday it had some substantial political victories. In the early 1900s, socialists captured 1,000 state and local offices around the country, including dozens of positions in state legislatures. Socialists even became mayors in a number of cities. Daniel Hoan, the socialist mayor of Milwaukee, was so successful that he served in office for 24 years (1916–1940) and the city was known as one of the best-governed municipalities in the country.[3] What did city-level "sewer socialism" look like? Here's how political science professor Peter Dreier describes it:

Under the Socialists, Milwaukee gained a reputation as a well-managed municipality. They believed that government had a responsibility to promote the common good, but particularly to serve the needs of the city's working class. They built community parks, including beautiful green spaces and recreation areas along the lakefront that are still widely-used. They increased the citywide minimum wage (28 years before the federal government adopted the idea) and established an eight-hour day standard for municipal workers. They championed public education for the city's children, built excellent libraries and sponsored vibrant recreation programs. The city municipalized street lighting, the stone quarry, garbage disposal and water purification.[4]

This gives us a place to start in thinking about the question of what it actually means for an elected official to be a "socialist." What is the political tradition that unites Berger and AOC, what makes them different from typical congressional members of the Democratic Party?

The word "socialism" can be difficult to define. Historian G. D. H. Cole's multivolume *History of Socialist Thought* begins by acknowledging that socialists have used the word to mean different things. We might begin by defining it as a kind of strong egalitarian political instinct that emphasizes "solidarity" with the working class against wealthy owners of capital. Even though the range of people who have called themselves "socialists" spans from mayor of Milwaukee Daniel Hoan to Vladimir Lenin to Alexandria Ocasio-Cortez, they share an identification with the people who have the least against the people who have the most.

This "working-class solidarity" is explicitly where Ocasio-Cortez herself locates her socialism. For example, when Uber was revealed to have maintained separate bathrooms for its drivers and its full-time employees, AOC slammed the company, saying the practice was "what classism looks like." This kind of class consciousness can be rare even among Democrats. AOC, when asked about the formation of her politics, talks about her personal experiences as the child of working-class parents, and her awareness of other people's economic struggles during the Great Recession. In the first major profile of AOC, written by Aída Chávez and Ryan Grim in *The Intercept* in June 2018, Ocasio-Cortez spoke movingly about how her political values were informed by what she had witnessed during her own upbringing, including her family's financial struggles after the death of her father:

> As the economy collapsed, she found herself "deeper and deeper underwater," she said. Her family became locked in a years-long probate battle with the Westchester County Surrogate's Court, which processes the estates of people who died without a will, as Ocasio-Cortez's father had. She witnessed firsthand how attorneys appointed by the court to administer an estate can enrich themselves at the expense of the families struggling to make sense of the bureaucracy. The family was barely getting by on her mom's income as a housecleaner and bus driver, and after Ocasio-Cortez graduated in 2011, she began bartending and waitressing to pitch in . . . Back in New York, she was fighting to stave off the banks, which were eyeing the family home. "We just couldn't afford to keep our home, and we had bankers going up to the curb of our home and taking photos of our house."[5]

Critics often describe "socialism" as "government control of production."[6] But what more frequently unites socialists is having had experiences like AOC's, sharing in a common struggle to survive and then developing a sense of outrage at preventable injustice. Millennial socialists are often college educated and came of age during the financial crisis; they watched their peers and their families work hard and get little in return. Even when they have middle-class backgrounds, they are frequently people who have had personal exposure to the ways in which the "American dream" is a myth in an age of colossal inequality.

AOC was not a child of privilege who read Marx and had a revelation about economic theory, though she does have a degree in economics. Instead, she was someone who became outraged as she saw a small class of people becoming ever more rich while working people in Queens and the Bronx could not afford housing or health care. AOC has been quite explicit that by "socialism" she means "worker power," not "government ownership":

Socialism does not mean government owns everything. I disagree with that notion as well because I think it is undemocratic. I think that it is very easily corrupted and I don't think that that's a good thing. But I do think that having more democracy in our economy, aka worker power, worker accountability, is a very positive thing.

What does she mean by "worker power"? In part, it means aggressive support for labor unions. When a solar energy company fired workers attempting to unionize, AOC publicly demanded the workers be rehired.[7] When Barstool Sports founder Dave Portnoy threatened to crush any unionizing efforts at his company, AOC told him that he might face legal action.[8] Her Green New Deal plan emphasizes worker rights and working conditions as well as environmental mitigation, including specific provisions about the quality of jobs that the Green New Deal should guarantee and a demand that those jobs be unionized.[9]

Socialists have always paid close attention to the relative amounts of power possessed by ordinary workers and business owners. Support for labor unions is an important part of democratic socialist politics not just because labor unions secure workers higher pay and better benefits, but because they reduce the power of employers to arbitrarily fire and coerce employees.[10] This is the reasoning behind proposals like Bernie Sanders's "workplace democracy" and "corporate accountability and democracy" plans.[11] The workplace democracy plan bans firing for any reason other than "just cause," makes it easier to form a union, and eliminates "right-to-work" laws that ban mandatory union membership.[12] The corporate democracy plan would distribute shares of large corporations to employees and mandate that 45 percent of corporate board members be directly elected by employees. (This kind of scheme, called "codetermination," already exists in Germany and is considered successful.)[13] None of these things turns the United States "socialist," but all of them embody the democratic socialist conviction that bosses and owners should have less power relative to ordinary workers.

Importantly, this shows why critics are wrong to conceive of socialists as primarily aiming for "government control," even though socialists do often advocate a greater role for government. In fact, government is simply used as a means to an end: as an institution owned by all, with accountability through elections, government is the vehicle through which we can enact our collective aspirations. For an issue like climate change, government is the only institution with both the power and the level of popular control necessary to address the problem at sufficient scale. AOC's goal is not state power but worker power, some of which might come through nationalizing industries, but some that might come by redistributing corporate ownership to ordinary laborers instead of rich shareholders. In that case, the government's job is to create laws that restructure companies, but the ultimate *power* is being given to working people rather than the state.

AOC's socialism certainly involves a skepticism of private corporations. Though she talks about the need to be cautious in empowering government, her main fear is of the dangers that corporate profit seeking poses. For example, *Newsweek* reported on an explanation of socialism Ocasio-Cortez gave during an Instagram livestream:

Ocasio-Cortez said there are sectors where the profit motive should be removed and that, at the very least, a public option should always be available. She used America's public school system as an example. "Imagine if we had to pay tuition for our kids to go to school from kindergarten all the way through twelfth grade. It would be untenable, unfeasible, and we would have to rely on businesses that are always trying to profiteer," she said. "Imagine if Walmart ran your public school. That does not sound fun at all. And so, some people are able to send their kids to private schools. You can do that if that's what you want to do. If you want to pay $30,000 to send your kid to kindergarten, which some people do in New York City, that's your business. But we as a society have decided that it is important and that it is vital enough that we provide a public option for elementary education in the United States," she said, adding that the U.S. military is the "original federal jobs guarantee."[14]

Profit is often seen as a good or neutral force, even among Democrats. Larry Summers, the director of Barack Obama's National Economic Council, said that even liberal economists were now all "Friedmanites," referring to the conservative economist Milton Friedman. Friedman famously wrote that "the social responsibility of business is to increase its profits," meaning that the pursuit of private profit would always serve the ultimate social good. Ocasio-Cortez forcefully rejects this idea as applied to schooling. While she does not specify the exact role she *does* envision for profit, she makes it clear that there are spheres where it should not govern. This is rhetoric that harkens back to an older form of leftism and an older kind of rhetoric that has been little heard in the business-friendly "school reform" movement.

Whether this is "anti-capitalism" is open for question. Certainly, Bernie Sanders rejects the term, and AOC herself does not identify—as Elizabeth Warren does—as a "capitalist to her bones." But what is the vision toward which Ocasio-Cortez and Sanders aspire? Is it simple Scandinavian social democracy or something greater? In some ways, that question is deceptive: in the United States, having Scandinavian social democracy would be quite radical. Countries like Finland and Norway have far higher levels of public ownership, far more social benefits, far less inequality, and far more leisure than the United States does. They are often identified as "capitalist" countries, but they do have many more "socialized" institutions: a much more robust public sector and greater embodiment of the socialist principle "from each according to their ability, to each according to their need." *Because* the United States is so far from achieving even this modest, eminently realizable social democratic society, it is perhaps premature to ask questions about how much "further" AOC and Sanders would go once that vision is achieved. For the moment, it is enough to say that their socialism would create a very different kind of American economy from the one we have now, one that would be far more egalitarian and humane.

AOC asks questions that rarely get asked in Washington. For instance, in the above passage, she asks us to imagine what it would be like if we didn't have public elementary schools, and students had to take on debt like they do for college. In doing so, she makes the case for why college itself should be free: if it would be absurd for students to take on debt to go to high school, why is it not absurd for the next level of education?

That willingness to radically question common assumptions, and challenge prevailing orthodoxies, is just as important a part of AOC's socialism as any economic theory. Prior to AOC, what member of Congress would ever have tweeted positively about the idea of abolishing prisons altogether?[15] Who would have dared to compare America's border prisons to "concentration camps"?[16] Who would have said that the very existence of billionaires presents a moral problem?[17] Who would have confronted the super-rich in such a direct and uncompromising way? These are bold departures from the political norm, and they show that AOC's socialism is not just a new label but an authentic new kind of radicalism.

Consider, too, the legislation AOC is working on. Her "A Just Society" legislation of six bills included national caps on rent increases, the expansion of federal benefits to undocumented immigrants and people with criminal records, and the granting of federal contracts to companies that offer a $15 minimum wage and paid family leave.[18] Her Green New Deal explicitly linked the fight against climate change with broader fights for social and economic justice.[19] Her brand of environmentalism is explicitly "socialist," in that when she talks about climate change she also talks about poverty and working people. Responding to a charge that the environment was an "elitist" issue, Ocasio-Cortez was furious:

> This is not an elitist issue. This is a quality of life issue. You want to tell people that their concern and their desire for clean air and clean water is elitist? Tell that to the kids in the South Bronx which are suffering from the highest rates of childhood asthma in the country. Tell that to the families in Flint whose kids, their blood is ascending in lead levels, their brains are damaged for the rest of their lives. Call them elitist. You're telling them that those kids are trying to get on a plane to Davos? People are dying![20]

This kind of deep concern with the lived experiences of poor people is rarely heard in Washington. Nor do we often hear this kind of *anger*. Democratic socialism, for Ocasio-Cortez, is not just about economics but about a willingness to get out in the streets, to march alongside activists, and to position herself on the side of the people rather than fellow politicians. One of her first acts after being elected was visiting with environmental activists who were occupying Nancy Pelosi's office.[21] Ocasio-Cortez could have sided with Pelosi, the leader of her party. Instead, she made it clear that her sympathies were with the activists. She pursues an "inside-outside" strategy that sees social movements as equally important as government and believes that political institutions depend on popular pressure for their success.

AOC has professed herself dissatisfied with incrementalism and sees political challenges as urgent enough to require radical departures from existing norms. This involves more transformative legislation and even a willingness to challenge fellow members of her party. One does not have to be a democratic socialist to hold this position, but it *is* the case that even many "progressive" Democrats like Barack Obama and Nancy Pelosi, who do not consider themselves to be in the conservative wing of their party, have shown a much greater desire for party unity than the left has. The Democratic Congressional Campaign Committee has made it clear that it sees people like AOC as enemies—the DCCC has warned that it will blacklist any firm or vendor that supports primary challengers to Democratic incumbents.[22]

That is a core way in which AOC sets herself apart. Like Bernie Sanders, she has disdain for the "party establishment," and she does not believe in respecting Democrats just because they have a "D" next to their name. After all, that is why she ran for office in the first place. Joe Crowley was not necessarily a *terrible* Democrat, but he was someone she felt had completely lost touch with his constituents and who didn't feel the kind of urgency that she felt was so desperately needed. As she said of him:

> Americans, they hear the name Joe Crowley and they say, "Who?" . . . And that's been out of his playbook this entire time. If you look at his career as an assemblyman, people were like, "Who is this guy?" He really had no legislative triumphs as an assemblyman. He was kind of like a shadowy figure; he never came out in support of anything bold.[23]

That "boldness," the willingness to question existing practices, is a hallmark of her politics. When she got to Washington, AOC decreed that her staff would all earn a living wage of $52,000, breaking with others in her party who paid low salaries.[24] She quickly developed a reputation as a combative questioner in hearings and was willing to challenge the CEOs of giant corporations over their harmful practices in a tone of populist indignation rarely heard on Capitol Hill.[25] On Twitter, she mocked and derided companies like Amazon for mistreating their workers and issued statements of support for workers taking on their bosses.[26] When Fox News criticized her for being too harsh on billionaires, she posted screenshots and laughed.[27] She even exposed "dirty secrets" of how Congress worked, such as the indoctrination seminar freshman House members are given at Harvard (she called it a "lobbyist project" that promotes a corporate agenda), and the way homeless people are paid to stand in line for hearings so that lobbyists don't have to.[28]

It's a brash and refreshing approach, one rarely seen in the halls of power. When Stephen Colbert asked AOC how many "fucks she gave," her answer was "0," and every day she has shown she means it.[29]

Of course, many reformers mellow once they get into power, and those on the left who admire AOC sometimes worry that she will succumb to political pressure to moderate her positions. It appears that the Democratic Party leadership forced her to get rid of her outspoken chief of staff, Saikat Chakrabarti, and she has sometimes made statements that have ruffled leftist supporters (for example, walking back her previous criticism of Israel in an interview on *Firing Line*, and suggesting that socialism and capitalism might be compatible).[30] A cynic might expect that AOC would follow the well-traveled path from "youthful radicalism" to "acceptance of the status quo" as she finds out "how Washington really works" and "learns to make compromises." If that is indeed what happens, it would be disappointing, because AOC is remarkable and compelling precisely because of her "youthful radicalism" and her refusal to make the usual compromises. She is independent minded, daring, and says what has been on the minds of many but too few have been willing to say. If she tones it down, we will all be poorer for it.

But it does not appear as if AOC plans to tone it down

anytime soon. She recently made a clear new statement of her political allegiance by endorsing Bernie Sanders's presidential campaign and has frequently given her support to left challengers to Democratic establishment figures (for instance, by supporting "Medicare for All" champion Abdul El-Sayed in his progressive gubernatorial campaign in Michigan).[31] She has aligned herself with Justice Democrats and Brand New Congress, who are openly trying to replace centrist Democrats with a crop of young radicals. And while she has recognized that she sometimes has to make nice with party leaders like Nancy Pelosi if she is to get along in Washington, she continues to stir the pot and show a willingness to generate outrage when her cause is just.

If we are to think about what "democratic socialism" means to Ocasio-Cortez, a strong clue comes from the speech Bernie Sanders gave at the rally where AOC endorsed him. Speaking about the need for leftists to show solidarity with others who do not share their personal troubles, Sanders echoed sentiments that AOC herself has expressed many times:

> I want you all to take a look around and find someone you don't know, maybe somebody who doesn't look kind of like you, who might be of a different religion, maybe who come from a different country . . . My question now to you is, are you willing to fight for that person who you don't even know as much as you're willing to fight for yourself? . . . Are you willing

to fight to ensure that every American has health care as a human right, even if you have good health care? Are you willing to fight for frightened immigrant neighbors, even if you are native born? Are you willing to fight for a future for generations of people who have not yet even been born, but are entitled to live on a planet that is healthy and habitable? Because if you are willing to do that, if you are willing to fight for a government of compassion and justice and decency, if you are willing to stand up to Trump's desire to divide us up, if you are prepared to stand up to the greed and corruption of the corporate elite, if you and millions of others are prepared to do that, there is no doubt in my mind that not only will we win this election, but together we will transform this country.

This is an expression of a kind of "intersectional socialism," one that ties together the fights for racial justice, gender justice, environmental justice, and economic justice. It is a philosophy that does not put "class issues" before other issues but that sees all issues as part of one giant social struggle. I do not think it is coincidental that Sanders expressed this idea most clearly at the event where he was endorsed by AOC, because it is the kind of socialism that AOC herself has been majorly responsible for developing and articulating.

One more aspect of AOC's politics is worth mentioning. Her socialism is about elevating ordinary people, and as part of that, she has also foregrounded her own ordinariness. She has shown a willingness to expose her human side, whether by dancing outside her office or having fun with a penguin or getting licked by a dog.[32] She embodies a deep "anti-elitist" philosophy, one that says: *You should not have to be privileged and have an Ivy League education to serve in government. It is okay if you are an ordinary working person. If I can do it, so can you.* There is a kind of "uplifting of ordinariness" in Ocasio-Cortez's willingness to show anger, humor, sadness, and joy. She is a person who remembers where she came from, and who invites all of us to enter the halls of power and says that we belong there.

When Ocasio-Cortez was elected, she posted an inspiring social media message about her background. She wrote:

Mami mopped floors, drove school buses, + answered phones. She did whatever she needed to do, for me. When my father died, she was left a single mother of 2, and again she had to start over. After he passed we almost lost our home, so we sold it and started over. & over. & over. It wasn't long ago that we felt our lives were over; that there were only so many do-overs until it was just too late, or too much to take, or we were too spiritually spent. I was scrubbing tables + scooping candle wax after restaurant shifts & falling asleep on the subway ride home. I once got pickpocketed, & everything I earned that day was stolen. That day I locked myself in a room and cried deep: I had nothing left to give, or to be. And that's when I started over. I honestly thought as a 28 year old waitress I was too late; that the train of my fulfilled potential had left the station.

Soon after thinking that the train of her potential had left the station, Ocasio-Cortez would become the youngest congresswoman in American history. And that is part of what is so radical, so socialist, about her presence in the House of Representatives. Through her achievement, she makes the impossible seem possible, the radical seem doable. She encourages us to dream big, to refuse to succumb to hopelessness. It is no wonder she is feared and hated by the right. Alexandria Ocasio-Cortez's democratic socialism is a threat to the established order, because she presents a vision of a possible politics where young people, working people, women, and people of color all create a humane and decent society together, one where everyone is clothed, housed, fed, and given quality health care, and you don't have to be a billionaire to serve in public office. She is threatening in part because she sees herself as part of a social movement, in which organized workers will come together to take back control over their lives. She is the expression of a profound and new kind of socialist politics, one that may very well change the world.

On Being an Indignant Brown Girl

Prisca Dorcas Mojica Rodriguez

Context: I do not believe in true objectivity, so before I start, I want to name my biases. We all have them whether we like to admit it or not . . .

The thing about American politicians, when you are an immigrant (or really anyone who is marginalized due to their race, class, gender, sexuality, and such), is that it is hard to fully trust them. A lot of immigrants, especially those who grew up in countries directly impacted by U.S. foreign policy and understand the circumstances of immigration, will resent politicians due to the impact their policies have had on their lives. As an immigrant, I regard a lot of our politicians with suspicion at best, straight-up anger at worst.

I come from a country that experienced a lot of wrong-doing at the behest of the United States. Empires are not built without the demise of other nations and the subjugation, whether forced or not, of smaller and less powerful countries. My country's government has been manipulated for years, and revolutions have been halted if they were perceived as a threat to U.S. companies.

My own family has a long history of fallen soldiers, fighting wars both for our government and for the revolution. Both sides were set up to fail, because they were not fighting one another, they were fighting the wealthy and political elites of the United States of America. Trauma is inherited, and survival instincts are passed down.

The USA placed an embargo on my country on May 1, 1985.

> I, Ronald Reagan, President of the United States of America, find that the policies and actions of the Government of Nicaragua constitute an unusual and extraordinary threat to the national security and foreign policy of the United States and hereby declare a national emergency to deal with that threat.[1]

Embargos withhold incoming goods and resources, making modern-day living hard. And the thing about an embargo placed by a powerful country like the United States is that it not only stops goods and resources coming from the USA, but it also stops goods and resources coming from allied countries.

I was born three months later, on August 11, 1985.

Even stuff like camera film was difficult to obtain under this embargo, and therefore there are gaps in my childhood pictures. Stories are told and retold, but there is a barrier between me and those who have been fortunate enough to have their memories captured—without gaps. There is an additional conversation to be had. It can either be an engaged and exhaustive discussion regarding oppression and colonialism, or a casual "I do not have a lot of pictures of my childhood."

Things like this shape and change people. There is a difference between thriving and surviving. I grew up in a country that the USA coerced into doing what the USA thought was best for the USA.

So, I view politicians with suspicion. I do not trust that what they are doing is entirely well-intentioned, and I do not automatically assume that they would care about my humanity if I was not a person residing in the United States of America. But because I hold multitudes inside of me, I am also a person who follows politics.

So, all that to say: Bow down.

I, like many others around the country, was intrigued when a brown Latina from the Bronx beat a white man. Alexandra Ocasio-Cortez came alive to me on the day that she became a household name; women who cannot be contained need to see one another existing and thriving.

When I first saw her live, there was something in her

eyes I could not name, but that I now realize is audacity. She has to be bold to step into a modern-day version of one of Dante's circles of hell, where the patriarchy of this country is bred: Washington, D.C.

So I say again: Bow down.

When Trump dismissed her, and many other straight white male cis politicians and anchor hosts came out and denounced things she said, it not only confirmed my suspicion of politicians but also set AOC apart for me in the ways that I did not know I needed her to be set apart. She suddenly reminded me of all the brave women I know, who are audacious and bold. For me, AOC went from being a politician, flawed and carrying a long-treacherous international legacy, to being an audacious Latina who was not going to sit and let these powerful men continue to fuck with her, and us. A woman who defends herself and those who need her advocacy, who doesn't function to defend or uphold white supremacy and the patriarchy, is powerful.

A series of recent events made me take further notice; confirming what I saw in her. At the House Oversight hearing on "The Trump Administration's Child Separation Policy: Substantiated Allegations of Mistreatment," AOC said:

> It is unnecessary to have a policy that calls children unaccompanied when they arrive with older brothers, sisters, and grandparents; and treat them no differently than human traffickers.

I felt advocated for because our *gente* are suffering at the border, and she is one of the few voices talking boldly about it. While racist Twitter called the groups of desperate immigrants "hordes of zombies," AOC brought humanity back into the conversation, and while radically right xenophobes vilified these hungry and helpless families, AOC rightfully vilified our own government for turning their backs on the crisis at the border.

AOC dares to not seek approval; rather, she seeks justice. Women like this exist despite the socialization of girlhood/womanhood which teaches and rewards meekness and deference. Women like this exist despite constantly being told to simmer down and "stay in their lanes." Women like this cannot be contained.

Witness: AOC asked Mark Zuckerberg:

You would say white supremacist–tied publications meet a rigorous standard for fact-checking?

I am a millennial and I understand, revere, and fear the tech industry. We are all aware of how much of ourselves is sold to companies, including all the information we give freely; that our manipulation and exploitation by social media giants like Facebook is grotesque, at best. When I saw this live feed through my laptop I stopped working and turned the volume up. AOC not holding back any punches when speaking to one of the heavyweights in tech was thrilling. And when I saw Zuckerberg fumble, I felt that too. I felt the power of AOC's question. Questioning mega-powerful men in the ways AOC does is powerful because *she looks like me.*

She and I are both indignant brown girls.

Being an indignant brown girl is hard; I struggle with what it means to be this way. Your friend circles are small, because other women and femmes inflict horizontal violence by correcting our "out of line" behaviors. Being this type of woman is lonely, and strength is assumed, but never softness—something we can also possess. That's why I created Latina Rebels. I wanted a place where I as a Latina could exist in all my fullness. I wanted to speak Spanish in posts if I felt like it, without translating. I wanted to curse because cursing felt powerful. I wanted a space in which I did not have to apologize.

Being an indignant brown girl means that even family turns their back on you because you shame them. You dare to say too much and exist too boldly; my family has accused me of "misrepresenting" them. I wonder how often a corrupt and wealthy white man hears that from his family, I wonder how often he cries himself to sleep because his *papi* phoned to tell him that he's ashamed to call him family.

What AOC has said and done is not spectacular for a straight white cis man, but extraordinary for a woman of color.

The attacks on AOC make clear how society views in-dignant brown women. It takes a five-second Google search to find the disapproval that AOC garners. Trump himself took the time to call her out among other newly elected women of color in a series of racist tweets that said:

> So interesting to see "Progressive" Democrat Congress-women, who originally came from countries whose governments are a complete and total catastrophe . . . viciously telling the people of the United States, the greatest and most powerful Nation on earth, how our government is to be run. Why don't they go back and help fix the totally broken and crime infested places from which they came.

What AOC has said about the USA is not untrue nor is it unfounded, yet here Trump manages to absolve the USA of any wrongdoing and "others" AOC, a citizen of this country, by telling her and the other women of color that they do not get to have a say in what other straight white cis men like him built.

The day I saw Trump publicly disrespect AOC and tweet racist vitriol, I suddenly felt a need to protect her. When I read his tweets, I felt triggered because the idea that we must "go back to our countries" when we seek to improve the country we call home *is* xenophobia. Trump is implying that if we don't look like them then we must not be American. But the USA would not be the USA without immigration, and let's not forget that the white people of this country are really just land-grabbers who stole from the brown indigenous people who ruled the Americas long before white men came.

The world is cruel to brilliant women. Learning to step into the lack of acceptance, lack of sympathy, and cruelty of this straight white cis USA is hard, and learning to do it on a national scale with national attention seems overwhelming.

When AOC responded to Trump's tweet and said:

You are angry because you can't conceive of an America that includes us.

I felt that. I felt that in every inch of my body, because she said what many women of color have wanted to say but have been afraid to because of the possible consequences including outright shunning. AOC needs to be protected because AOC is all the women who dare to believe they are the most brilliant person in a room, even when the room is full of men. But we know that women of color are shunned in almost all industries, and never considered sufficiently smart or competent. This is a product of racism, classism, and sexism, and that intersection cannot be overlooked when we talk about AOC.

I remember the first time I witnessed a straight white

man talk about how "stupid" AOC is. I had seen the tweets and I had heard the news anchors on Fox, and I think I had come to expect that to a certain extent. Men have belittled my intelligence; I have dared to know more and I have been shamed for it by teachers, lovers, and even my own *papi*. But I never even considered that others would try to invalidate AOC by coming for her intelligence. I have seen politicians do and say idiotic things, and I have long thought that being smart was not even a primary qualification for the job. Sometimes it has felt like becoming president of the United States is just about having money. But AOC is very well-read and has been exposed to both the sciences and the social sciences, and has a real comprehensive view of the things she is passionate about. So, I repeat, it never occurred to me that she is unintelligent, though it instantly occurred to many straight white cis men.

I am brilliant, beautiful, and unstoppable and I owe nothing to men—to any man.

Scratch that, men inspire me. Men inspire this fire and this anger, men inspire this audacity. All they ever taught me was that I was brilliant only when I was affirmed by them, beautiful only when I was catcalled and thus approved by the male gaze, and unstoppable only if they did not stand in my way.

As a society, we have a huge disdain for women who unapologetically live into their own power, women who self-determine. We like words like *compromise* and *reconciliation* and *unity*. But I need to sit in full admiration of my prowess without having to apologize to any man for my words. I need to hold my power and my voice and gawk at it, love it, because it has been long overdue. And not only do I need to do that, I need to see that done by other women to even imagine that possibility.

Being an indignant brown girl means partners try to tame you. I am a hurricane, a fuckin' tsunami, and a tornado, all in one. I am intense and passionate, and I will demand intensity. And when I do not get what I want from my male partner, I leave them on the side of the road, without any regard. I can forget you. Believe me when I say that I will never look back.

AOC, your laughter carries liberation in it, and your indignation at injustice inspires us. May the cackles of our unified laughter spark the way for other women to set themselves free! Women like us may be difficult to love; but may we learn to love ourselves enough for all the doubters.

Making the Green New Deal the Real Deal

Elizabeth C. Yeampierre

I imagine Puerto Rican radical mothers across New York City sat on the edge of their sofas experiencing excitement and ownership when Alexandria Ocasio-Cortez won the democratic primary in June 2018, ensuring her election to the U.S. Congress. I know I did. Just a few years before, I was brimming with pride at the appointment of Supreme Court justice Sonia Sotomayor, but this was different. AOC could be my daughter. She embodies the kind of leadership we dream of: brilliant, courageous, and gifted, with a quick mind and an understanding of our history and the political moment from which she emerged. And most importantly to me, she believes in environmental justice.

The climate justice leadership, of which I'm a member, is an intergenerational group of national frontline leaders who grew up fighting petrochemical industries, power plants, waste transfer stations, and fracking because these polluters—discriminately sited in our communities—were killing us. As part of that leadership, I was eager to sit down with Congresswoman Ocasio-Cortez to talk about the legacy and transformational work of our frontline-led members to ensure climate justice. I wanted to explain what we mean by a Just Transition—the move away from an extractive, fossil fuel–dependent economy to one based on renewable energy. We focus on local issues, from food security to community-owned solar cooperatives. I thought Alexandria could help lift up the narrative of frontline environmental justice activism and give it the attention it so desperately deserves at this critical time.

I didn't come to this work with a degree in environmental policy. It happened organically: as a child, my family was displaced so often that I went to eight schools in five years. I remember walking past the burning embers on Simpson Street in the South Bronx. I had no idea then that we were living in the midst of brownfields, contaminated lots with lead, asbestos, PCBs, arsenic, and other toxics and toxicants that seeped through our walls as fugitive dust and landed in our developing lungs. Families like mine all over New York City were the targets of government—and developer-driven—planned shrinkage public policies created to deny our communities basic services in order to encourage our departure. The New York City environmental justice movement was born and raised in the midst of this rubble. My father died of an asthma attack in his early fifties and I suffered a severe bilateral pulmonary embolism that almost took me too. It was clear to us that we could not fight for social justice if we did not address the most fundamental right—our right to breathe.

Sadly, my personal journey is common in poor, working-class communities of color all over the nation. Add the growing climate crises to this toxic soup that we have endured for generations and we are on what is called the frontline of the climate crisis.

My organization, UPROSE, is a community-based organization in Sunset Park, Brooklyn, that advocates for just, sustainable economic development and environmental justice. Our advocacy for climate justice is rooted in our struggles against displacement—displacement by rising waters and rising costs of living, worsened by the commercial speculation in our industrial neighborhood.

I grew up in a home where my grandmother reused, recycled, and repurposed out of necessity. Our knowledge of and our historical relationship with Mother Earth make us frontline people the least responsible for climate change. We have always lived sustainably. And we carry the struggle of our families and our ancestors into this work.

So I called AOC's office to discuss the need to center frontline solutions and climate justice and was surprised when her staff scheduled a phone call without hesitation. I felt proud; it appeared we were both excited to meet each other. I wondered, though, whether she was what she seemed.

After our introduction, I spent an hour breaking down the environmental justice movement (which has been around for decades). I tried to cram everything I knew into our call. I suggested she speak to Indigenous leaders fighting pipelines in Indian Country and frontline communities in the Gulf South, farmers in Puerto Rico, and activists in Detroit. I wanted her to know we were organized, and represented communities all over the country. I asked her to lead on climate justice. It was important that she understand the distinction between the climate movement and those of us from frontline communities that fought at the intersection of racial injustice and climate change. Climate solutions, for example, can become environmental justice problems. You can't focus on reducing carbon without addressing the co-pollutants that have created health disparities in our communities.

Alexandria told me that she had attended a Hurricane Maria rally organized by UPROSE and had heard me speak. She had been in the audience anonymously, taking it all in. Among the campaigns we discussed at that rally was the Just Recovery work, which led to the creation of #OurPowerPRnyc an initiative responding to the needs of our members in Puerto Rico.

The Puerto Rican diaspora in New York City wanted to ensure that support went to the neediest people in Puerto Rico, given the island's current and past colonial status and the negative impact of the usurious debt, the austerity, and neglect of public services secured by PROMESA (the Puerto Rico Oversight, Management, and Economic Stability Act).

Puerto Rico was slowly surfacing from the devastation of Hurricane Maria in 2017. The United States' neglect during this unparalleled crisis contributed to the increased fragility of the island's ability to respond to the earthquakes that followed in 2019. As an activist I recognize the enormous impact caused by climate change on frontline communities everywhere. But my years working in the climate justice movement had not prepared me for Hurricane Maria's devastation and the impact it would have on our people on the island and in the diaspora and in my heart. I remember the call from my mom when she saw the footage of Hurricane Maria's impact. My mom has never had an easy life, but it was the first time I ever heard her cry, and all I remember was her saying I had to do everything I could to help Puerto Rico. It was so personal.

I explained to AOC that climate change was impacting the people least responsible for its creation. I spoke about New Orleans and the Gulf South and how the homes of the people displaced by Katrina were replaced by gentrifiers, speculators, and land grabbers who saw disaster as an opportunity. I talked about how FEMA had failed the frontline in the Gulf South, and how it was failing Puerto Rico. Even if FEMA was able to return a community to the way it was before a disaster it was still leaving it vulnerable—no steps were being taken to address the consequences of historical and institutional racism. She listened, took notes, asked questions, and shared her enthusiasm about working with the climate justice movement. I had no idea at that point that others had already tapped her to lead on what would be known far and wide as "the Green New Deal," or "GND."

Not long after our meeting, I was surprised when the Green New Deal exploded on the national stage and saturated social media. The idea moved fast, and in so doing, it raised questions about where it originated, why the majority of those living on the frontlines of the climate crisis had not been consulted, and what it meant for our communities. After all, AOC knew about us and was familiar with our principles and our work.

We soon learned that Alexandria was being courted and briefed by new and old "big green" organizations with a history of treating our communities as their poster children. Some academics and climate change die-hards were quick to condemn the questions we were raising as unnecessary and time-consuming distractions, blocking the creation of ideas big enough to address the urgency and size of the crises.

As part of the leadership of the Climate Justice Alliance, which represents seventy organizations throughout the United States, I felt uniquely positioned to check in with our members about the proposed Green New Deal resolution. The national response was unanimous: no one had been consulted. I was disappointed to learn that the Green New Deal was created for us, but without us. As we do with any policy recommendation crafted without the engagement of those impacted, we had a responsibility to examine the GND and respond accordingly.

The Climate Justice Alliance convened a Green New Deal working group. We concluded that the GND did not center Just Transition or frontline communities and that it included concerning and false cap-and-trade solutions in its repertoire. It seemed the power of celebrity behind the Green New Deal had birthed a new movement that was not grounded in communities, but in the age-old practice of "well-intentioned" environmentalists helicoptering in for photo ops and media moments to advance their solutions. We recognized that we needed all hands on deck; we had to address the challenges created by Green New Deal followers, whether intentional or not—who should have been working with us.

On December 10, 2018, we issued a national statement and platform to begin to change the parameters of the conversation.[1] It was imperative, we said, that special attention be paid to the highly impacted communities bearing the brunt of the impacts of the climate crisis. One month later, on January 10, 2019, we met with AOC and her chief of staff in Washington, D.C.

Our platform stated that any Green New Deal *must*: center a just transition; support the rights of workers; go beyond carbon neutral strategies to include all greenhouse gas emissions and co-pollutants; support renewable energy, not just "clean energy"; renounce the false promise of climate geoengineering; reinvest in community-controlled and cooperative enterprises; ensure free, prior and informed consent by Indigenous peoples; and develop a GND process that is "transparent, inclusive, and democratic."

We said that we no longer have time for incremental solutions. Our demand for climate justice and an immediate and just transition that addresses the social and economic injustices that underpin climate change must be centered in any Green New Deal.

To her credit, after meeting with our delegation, AOC and her staff agreed to change the language, the messaging, and the core values of the Green New Deal. This was a deep departure from conventional politics, one that reminded us that AOC is not your run-of-the-mill politician. It appeared she was a woman looking to do right by her people and willing to correct herself when her trajectory took off without them.

Months later, as lead organizer for #OurPowerPRnyc, housed at UPROSE, we facilitated a series of events to educate our community about climate justice and a Just Transition. We organized rallies and forums and marched in the historic Puerto Rican Day Parade in New York City. When we reached out to AOC to participate she immediately said yes. At a rally we were organizing in Union Square that marked the one-year anniversary of Hurricane Maria, she joined #OurPowerPRnyc onstage using language, concepts, and frameworks that came from the very people most impacted by climate disasters. It was an uncompromising, unapologetic demonstration of respect for our community. It was refreshing and offered hope in the midst of despair.

Today, there are many Green New Deals arising around the nation. The majority have been in process for years. Whether in New York State, the Gulf South, or Portland, Oregon, or elsewhere, we must continue to center the traditional ecological knowledge of our indigenous and African diaspora communities on the frontlines in deep ways, from start to finish.

AOC's humility and ability to recognize the gaps and problems, while also working in tandem with members of Congress like Ilhan Omar and Rashida Tlaib, who both have a history of engagement in environmental justice, has made it possible for us to work with her.

Climate change is unlike any other threat in our history. It will test us in unimaginable ways. It demands leadership that celebrates difference, sees the frontline as partners in decision-making, and is willing to exercise courage for all of us. This sister from the Bronx is what this moment demands.

The Hustle

María Cristina (MC) González Noguera

I have a picture that I've displayed in every office I have ever worked in. It's from the 1950s and shows Doña Fela, the first female mayor in Puerto Rico. Doña Felisa Rincón de Gautier was the mayor of San Juan, and the first woman mayor of any capital city in the Americas. Next to her is my grandfather, Jose Ramón Noguera; he and Doña Fela worked together. He eventually rose to be secretary of the treasury in Puerto Rico, and in this picture, they are outdoors, leaning on a building, talking. It's completely casual, but it's such an important picture for me, because Doña Fela was a huge role model of mine. In the 1930s, she fought for women's rights, particularly the right to vote, and was the fifth woman to officially register to vote on the island once the law was passed. She advocated for the poor and helped implement groundbreaking public services, including preschool programs and centers for the elderly, and a reworking of the public health system. My grandfather was very supportive of her; he believed in public policy and in making sure that the right structures are in place so that everyone has opportunity. And he was very pro–female leadership. My grandfather had six granddaughters, and he wanted them all to be productive and valued, like the mayor was.

Fast-forward to 1980, when I was five years old and my mother decided to move us from Puerto Rico to Connecticut. She had just received her master's in social work, and a nonprofit in New London, Centro de la Comunidad, offered her a job helping Puerto Ricans coming from the island access the services available to them. We moved to Connecticut so my mother could put her master's to work, but I know she also wanted to make sure I had another role model; she wanted to model a working, independent woman for me. I'm grateful to my mom, because I learned so much from her through all those years that I still keep with me as an adult. I always remember her humor, her drive, her ambition. The hustle. My mom is five feet of hustle. In 1980, when her friends were all married and had these very traditional homes in Puerto Rico, she thought, *I have got to leave this island; I have to demonstrate to my daughter that there is more opportunity, and that there is a way to get at that opportunity, and that she has to go for it. And I have to practice what I preach.*

When I started school in New London, I didn't speak any English, and most of the other kids had been born and raised in Connecticut. But I was lucky enough to find another wonderful woman role model in my kindergarten teacher. As soon as she picked up on the fact that I didn't speak English, she didn't dwell on it and found other ways to connect with me knowing that in short order I would pick up the language. Similarly, my mother reassured me that New London was our new home and that I would quickly make friends and adapt. Their message was clear—persevere. Having those two adults providing me with that help made me feel so valued and supported.

But through all that time in our new place, it was my mom who was the most amazing influence. I have been lucky enough in my career to have held high-level positions in more than one profession, and I didn't even start out knowing what I wanted to do! While I was still in college I thought I might want to be a teacher, but my mother, having been a teacher herself, gently let me know that if I wanted to become a teacher, it would be an excellent choice, but that she believed I could do something else. She was the one who really pushed me to think about other avenues. After college, I started as an analyst in investment banking, then I moved to a communications firm in Washington, D.C. Next I worked in corporate communications for the Estée Lauder Companies. And from there, I landed at the White House to be First Lady Michelle Obama's communications director—before coming back to ELC.

When I think about my time in the White House, I still pinch myself. I still cannot believe that I had that opportunity, because . . . *yo soy la hija de Cristy y Min*. I am the daughter of Cristy and Min. It was an amazing place to work, because there was a sense in that administration that anything was possible. And after working for such a strong, dynamic, intelligent woman as Mrs. Obama, I certainly left that White House feeling like everything was possible.

Fast-forward to 2018—my post–White House life. I first heard of AOC when she was running in her primary against Joe Crowley, and something about her immediately spoke to me. I am always inspired to see another woman, I am always inspired to see another Hispanic woman, and I am incredibly inspired to see a Puerto Rican woman working and accomplishing like AOC is doing. Because if you think about it, we come from an island of three million people, and so the fact that *estamos hasta en las sopas!*—we are even in the soups!—is a testament to who we are as a people. Puerto Ricans, as a culture, tend to be very humble, and we sometimes don't speak as loudly as we could, don't ask for as much as we deserve. Generations of Puerto Ricans, particularly those who came to the States in the bigger migrations, were quite humble. There was less of a push to be recognized for the hard work and the contributions that we were making to society. We were grateful for the opportunity. There is a lot of value in that humility, but I believe we have now evolved to the point where we are very much aware of our contributions to the United States. Whether it's serving in the armed forces, creating our role in the workforce, or shaping culture through the arts, creativity in the arts, politics and policy, and business, we are sitting at the table, and we want to be heard.

Thankfully, you don't see it as much in the younger generations—that kind of humility that leads you to ask for less than you deserve—and I noticed that immediately about AOC. She does what a lot of people her age do so well: She is not afraid to put words—strong words—to emotions, situations, and conditions, fair or unfair. She knows what issues to put forward, and she is relentless in placing them on the table and driving them, regardless of where they will land. Her articulation of her platform was what made me take notice.

But beyond that, what particularly resonated with me was that, along with her passion for issues such as income inequality and the environment, she is making equal room for her advocacy for Latinos, Puerto Ricans, and specifically her island—which makes it all the more important that she was elected to the House at this exact time. Puerto Rico's status as an unincorporated territory, or commonwealth, of the United States means it has no voting members of Congress and no senators, and its citizens can't vote for president. The United States took control of Puerto Rico in 1898, and since then, Puerto Rico has never been fully integrated into the country. The island has one non-voting resident commissioner in the House of Representatives. And because of that status, Puerto Rican politicians who live on the mainland and hold office in the States have made a tradition of making sure the island, given its minimal federal representation, is advocated for and given the aid and assistance that is not only promised but constitutionally mandated. These politicians, as well as their Puerto Rican constituents, still feel a living, breathing connection to the island, through family members who still live there and through the travel they may make back and forth. Even longtime residents on the mainland maintain they feel connected in a deep and meaningful way to the island and the culture. After Hurricane Maria, longtime Bronx congressman José Serrano told the *New York Times*, "I've often said that I represent two districts: one in the Bronx, and one that's Puerto Rico."

Crushing debt in Puerto Rico and the humanitarian crisis that was Hurricane Maria have made fighting for the issues that help the island more urgent, and at the same time that we have begun slowly losing the pioneers, the first generation of trailblazing Puerto Rican leaders who were elected to Congress and were active in our national policy-making. Luis Gutiérrez (D-IL), who was first elected to the House in 1993, spent his tenure advocating for immigrants and became one of the top national voices on the issue—but said on the one-year anniversary of Hurricane Maria that he would dedicate "the next chapter" of his life to recovery and improvement of the island. He retired from the House in 2018. Congressman José Serrano, in the House of Representatives since 1990, fought tirelessly alongside colleagues like Nydia Velázquez for more funding for Puerto

Rico post-hurricane, and announced in 2019 he would not run again. Velázquez, also a first-time Congress member in the class of '93, has remained as one of the most outspoken voices on the need for funding, aid, and wholesale attention to Puerto Rico since the hurricane.

These members have made an effort to make up for Puerto Rico's non-voting status, but the island has only benefited from this personal and passionate advocacy since 1971, when Herman Badillo, the first Puerto Rican elected to Congress, took to the floor in his first term to urge Congress to improve conditions there. Badillo, early in his career, also fought for the poor in his district and for more federal funding for New York's underprivileged neighborhoods. He arrived in New York just as the Great Migration was getting under way. Between the 1940s and 1960s, thousands of Puerto Ricans left the island in search of jobs and better economic opportunity. Badillo was elected just as Puerto Ricans began to have a significant impact in New York. These leaders all worked, during their terms, to further the fight for poor, inner-city communities in their districts *and* on the island.

Of the 43 Latino members in Congress after Hurricane Maria, only five were Puerto Rican, but those members, including Serrano, Gutíerrez, and Velázquez, came together to fight for aid and relief for the storm-ravaged island. They also criticized the Trump administration when they felt the funding it allocated was inadequate.

It now feels crucial to make sure these voices are at the

table and to have an Alexandria Ocasio-Cortez there to increase their number by one. Before leaders like these were elected, the infrastructure that was fighting for communities of color existed only around the legislature, not in it. Organizations like Unidos US (formerly National Council of La Raza) and similar groups advocated for policy, as opposed to taking part in it. They were one step removed. Representatives of color have increased, and now that *inner* layer exists. AOC is *at* the table, speaking loudly and nationally.

But of everything that spoke to me about Alexandria Ocasio-Cortez, the thing that connected perhaps most of all had nothing to do with politics. I immediately noticed the bond she seems to have with her mother. When she was sworn in to Congress, she brought her mother—and all her family—to the swearing-in at the Capitol. Family even flew in from Puerto Rico! That was a real, emotional moment for me. If you are from Puerto Rico, you understand this dynamic of big families. When I think about the accomplishments in my life, there are so many times that I would have loved to have had my extended family there with me.

I felt a connection to AOC that day, seeing her mother in that very public forum—a woman who, like my mother, clearly was not used to very public forums. One of the things my mother does for me, that I'm forever grateful for, is really ground me. My mother always reminds me that I am part of a bigger family, I am part of a bigger community, and I have to show up for that family and that community. And perhaps I'm projecting, but I get the sense that that's what AOC's mother does for her, as well. Women like Sonia Sotomayor and Alexandria Ocasio-Cortez, these female role models in our community, have said publicly and articulately that no one expected them to reach these heights—except their families. Their families expected more of them, and they wanted to rise up to meet those expectations.

I find that incredibly powerful. It shows all of us that when we are thrown into uncomfortable situations, we have the power to rise. You're worried you'll be made to feel you don't belong, but you still leave the family kitchen table. In my case, if you throw this girl from Puerto Rico into the corporate conference room on 59th Street and Fifth Avenue, it turns out it doesn't matter how much Estée Lauder lipstick I have or how at home this company makes me feel, there is still a portion of me that feels foreign. But still, I show up, because in that moment in that conference room, I am representing all of us. That's what Doña Fela did for women and for her island, even after retiring, when she served as the American goodwill ambassador for four U.S. presidents. And that is what Alexandria Ocasio-Cortez is doing for so many of us. We need to make sure we are always showing up, making room, widening the lane, and reminding everyone that we deserve to be there. Because we've worked really hard, and we've persevered. I've now added Alexandria Ocasio-Cortez to the long line of brave women in my life. I'm grateful she had the courage—and the hustle—to run.

About the Contributors

LYNDA LOPEZ is an Emmy Award–winning journalist and anchor at WCBS NewsRadio 880 in New York. She has anchored and reported for ABC News and WCBS TV, as well as anchoring newscasts for the Fox5 and My9 television stations in New York. A former contributor to *Latina Magazine*, *Glamour*, and *Glam Belleza Latina*, Lopez lives in New York City.

With his extraordinarily diverse skill set and wide-ranging talent in both comedy and drama, Emmy and Peabody Award–winning writer, actor, and producer KEEGAN-MICHAEL KEY is one of Hollywood's most in-demand forces. From his award winning show *Key & Peele* to the feature animations *The Lion King* and *Toy Story 4*, to his current turn as Meryl Streep's love interest in *The Prom*, Keegan redefines what it means to be a chameleon and multi-hyphenate in the worlds of film, television, and theater.

JENNINE CAPÓ CRUCET is the author of the novel *Make Your Home Among Strangers*, winner of the International

Latino Book Award and cited as a best book of the year by
the *Guardian*, NBC Latino, and the *Miami Herald*; and of
the story collection *How to Leave Hialeah*, which won the
Iowa Short Fiction Award and the John Gardner Fiction
Book Award. A contributing opinion writer for the *New
York Times* and a recipient of a PEN/O. Henry Award, she
is currently an associate professor of English and ethnic
studies at the University of Nebraska. Her latest book is the
essay collection *My Time Among the Whites: Notes from an
Unfinished Education.*

ANDREA GONZÁLEZ-RAMÍREZ is a New York City–based
journalist from Vega Alta, Puerto Rico. A senior writer at
GEN, a Medium publication, she is also an Ida B. Wells
fellow at Type Investigations. She reports on a wide array
of topics, including women in politics, reproductive rights,
immigration, gender-based violence, and LGBTQ+ issues.
Her work has appeared in Refinery29, NPR's Latino USA, *El
Diario Nueva York*, Centro Voices, and *Diálogo*, among others. In 2016, she launched Los Que Se Fueron, a collection
of interviews exploring what it means to be a young Puerto
Rican living stateside. González-Ramírez earned a master's of
journalism from the Craig Newmark Graduate School of
Journalism at the City University of New York. She graduated magna cum laude from the University of Puerto
Rico, Río Piedras Campus, with a degree in journalism
and sociology.

PATRICIA REYNOSO is a writer and beauty executive with over 20 years of industry experience, from editorial (beauty editor roles at *W, Ladies' Home Journal,* and *Glam Belleza Latina* magazines and co-author of a skincare book with famed dermatologist Dr. Fredric Brandt) to business (communications roles at Lancôme, La Mer, and Bobbi Brown) to digital (branded content at Hearst Media). Currently Reynoso is a director with the local and cultural relevancy team at the Estée Lauder Companies. Reynoso and her husband, Euclide, reside in New Jersey. Their twins, Brandon and Grace, are college sophomores.

PEDRO A. REGALADO is a Junior Fellow of the Society of Fellows at Harvard University. He researches the history of race, immigration, and capitalism in American cities during the twentieth century. He is currently working on a book about Latinx work in twentieth-century New York City. Regalado's writing has been featured in the *Washington Post, Boston Review, Chronicle of Higher Education, Journal of Urban History,* and *Planning Perspectives.* Born in the Dominican Republic, Pedro grew up in New York's Washington Heights.

REBECCA TRAISTER is writer at large for *New York* magazine. A National Magazine Award winner, she has written about women in politics, media, and entertainment from a feminist perspective for *The New Republic* and *Salon* and has also contributed to *The Nation, New York Observer, New York Times,* and the *Washington Post.* She is the author of *New York Times* bestsellers *Good and Mad, All the Single Ladies,* and the award-winning *Big Girls Don't Cry.* She lives in New York with her family.

Born in Lima, Peru, **NATALIA SYLVESTER** is the award-winning author of two novels for adults and a forthcoming young-adult novel. *Chasing the Sun* was named the Best Debut Book of 2014 by *Latinidad Magazine* and *Everyone Knows You Go Home* won an International Latino Book Award and the 2018 Jesse H. Jones Award for Best Work of Fiction from the Texas Institute of Letters. Her third novel, *Running,* was released in May 2020 from Clarion Books/ HMH. Natalia's essays have appeared in the *New York Times, Bustle, Catapult, Latina* magazine, and *McSweeney's.* She received a BA in creative writing from the University of Miami and now lives and writes in Texas.

ERIN AUBRY KAPLAN is a contributing writer to the *New York Times* opinion page and a former weekly op-ed columnist for the *Los Angeles Times,* the first African American in the paper's history to hold the position. She began working as a journalist in 1992 for the *Los Angeles Times,* for City Times, a section created in the aftermath of civil unrest to expand meaningful coverage of the central city. Kaplan is the author of *I Heart Obama* and *Black Talk,*

Blue Thoughts, and Walking the Color Line: Dispatches from a Black Journalista.

TRACEY ROSS is a director at PolicyLink, a national research and action institute advancing racial and economic equity, where she focuses on federal policy and narrative change. Most recently, she led the organization's All-In Cities initiative, working with cities across the country to adopt policies and practices to build strong cities for all. Prior to joining PolicyLink, Tracey worked at the Center for American Progress, focusing on urban poverty and environmental justice, and at Living Cities, supporting building a green economy. Tracey has been a guest on MSNBC and Al Jazeera English, and was a regular commentator for SiriusXM's *The Agenda*. Her writing has appeared in the *New York Times*, *Washington Post*, *Essence*, ThinkProgress, *Ebony*, and *The Nation*. Tracey began her career in the offices of Senator Hillary Rodham Clinton (D-NY) and Senator Ken Salazar (D-CO). She completed her master's in public affairs with a focus on urban policy and planning at Princeton University.

CARMEN RITA WONG is a writer, speaker, and, as CEO of Malecon Productions, an investor and advisor to women-owned businesses and productions. A former national television host, magazine advice columnist, and faculty professor at New York University, Carmen has also been a contributor to NBC, MSNBC, CNN, CBS, and ABC and has written for the *New York Times* and *O* magazine. She serves on the board of the Planned Parenthood Federation of America and The Moth, hosts a podcast, has published two novels, and is currently working on her fifth book, a memoir.

MARIANA ATENCIO is a Peabody Award–winning news personality, author, and public speaker, included in *Adweek*'s "Young Influentials" for 2019, as well as the founder of Go Like, her multimedia production company. She has covered domestic and international issues as an anchor and national correspondent on television for a decade, from breaking news to special reports in English and Spanish. Mariana's TEDx Talk on authenticity, "What Makes You Special?," has been viewed more than 10.5 million times and translated into ten languages. Her first book, *Perfectly You: Embracing the Power of Being Real*, was an Amazon #1 Best Seller for Hispanic & Latino Biographies. Its audio counterpart was also selected by Audible and Apple as a "Must Listen." As one of the few Latina storytellers currently on mainstream network news, she has become one of the most important voices in the Latinx community. Mariana came to the United States after losing the hope of becoming a journalist in her home country of Venezuela. Suddenly, as an immigrant and the new girl on television, she was faced with a choice: be what everybody else expected or find her own voice and purpose.

She realized that redefining herself beyond labels was the only way forward. She has reported from the trenches of the Venezuelan pro-democracy movement and has been at the forefront of the immigration debate in the United States. Her work has been honored with a Peabody, a Gracie, and an IRE award. In 2019, she won Columbia University Journalism School's First Decade Award and the National Association of Hispanic Journalists Presidential Award, and was nominated for a national Emmy. You can find her on all social media @marianaatencio.

WENDY CARRILLO was elected to serve in the California State Assembly in December 2017. She represents the 51st Assembly District in the City of Los Angeles and unincorporated East Los Angeles, which includes some of the most historic and iconic communities in the city. Prior to being elected to office, Assemblywoman Carrillo was a broadcast journalist for 12 years, covering human rights, global conflict, and U.S. politics. Assemblywoman Carrillo immigrated to the United States as a young child during El Salvador's civil war and is a first-generation American with Salvadoran and Mexican heritage.

NATHAN J. ROBINSON is a leading voice of millennial left politics. He is the editor of *Current Affairs*, a print magazine of political and cultural analysis. His work has appeared in the *New York Times, Washington Post, Guardian, The New Republic, The Nation,* and elsewhere. A graduate of Yale Law School, he is a Ph.D. student in sociology and social policy at Harvard University, where his work focuses on the U.S. criminal justice system. Nathan is the author of *Why You Should Be a Socialist.*

PRISCA DORCAS MOJICA RODRIGUEZ was born in Managua, Nicaragua, but calls Nashville, Tennessee, home. She has a Masters of Divinity from Vanderbilt University, has published over 200 articles, and participated in the Young Adult anthology *Nevertheless, We Persisted.* She founded the platform Latina Rebels in 2013, and has been featured in Telemundo, Univision, Mitú, Huffington Post Latino Voices, Guerrilla Feminism, *Latina Mag, Cosmopolitan,* and *Everyday Feminism.* She is at work on her first book with Seal Press, titled *Dear Woke Brown Girl.* She is unapologetic, angry, and uncompromising about protecting and upholding the stories of brown folks. *¡Que viva la gente!*

ELIZABETH C. YEAMPIERRE, Esq., is an internationally recognized Puerto Rican environmental/climate justice leader of African and Indigenous ancestry, born and raised in New York City. Elizabeth is co-chair of the Climate Justice Alliance and executive director of UPROSE, Brooklyn's oldest Latino community–based organization. Her award-winning vision for an intergenerational, multicultural, and community-led organization is the driving force behind UPROSE. Ms. Yeampierre was the first

Latina to chair the U.S. Environmental Protection Agency's National Environmental Justice Advisory Council (NEJAC). Her work led to the creation of a working group dedicated to developing recommendations for resilience for industrial waterfront communities. Ms. Yeampierre was also a member of the NIEHS National Advisory Environmental Health Sciences Council. Elizabeth was part of the national environmental justice leadership team to brief the Obama transition team in 2008. Elizabeth was selected as the opening speaker at the first White House Forum on Environmental Justice. Yeampierre is a member of the People's Climate March leadership team and a featured speaker at local, national, and international forums. Her work is featured in several books as well as in *Latina* magazine, *Vogue*, and a variety of other media outlets. Elizabeth was featured as one of 13 international climate warriors by *Vogue* magazine and was a speaker at Sage Paris and GRI 2016 in Amsterdam. She recently was named by Apolitical as part of the "Climate 100: The World's Most Influential People in Climate Policy" and was a recipient of the Frederick Douglass Abolitionist Award FD200.

MARÍA CRISTINA (MC) GONZÁLEZ NOGUERA is a seasoned communications executive currently serving as leader of a group at the Estée Lauder Companies that is responsible for global public affairs. Prior to that, Ms. González Noguera served as First Lady Michelle Obama's communications director in the White House. Previously,

Ms. González Noguera was a managing director for the Washington, D.C., strategic communications firm Chlopak, Leonard, Schechter & Associates (CLS). A native of San Juan, Puerto Rico, Ms. González Noguera is a graduate of Tufts University and a member of the Unidos US board of directors.

Acknowledgments

Sitting in a coffee shop one cold, windy February afternoon, I watched as a lovely, petite blond woman came walking toward my table carrying an armful of books. It was the first time I was getting to meet Elisabeth Dyssegaard, St. Martin's Press editor and good friend of one of my *amigas* (as well as one of my biggest mentors), Veronica Chambers. As Elisabeth and I talked, we began discussing the rise and impact of AOC. She told me about an idea she had for an anthology featuring powerful Latina voices, and I grew more excited the more we spoke about it: giving space to women of color to speak about one of our own. That afternoon led to this book, and I am forever grateful to Elisabeth for not only believing in me during this project, but for her unending patience, mentorship, and generosity throughout the whole process. I had never worked on a book, let alone an anthology, and her guidance through this project—along with her good heart and unwavering cheery disposition—were so appreciated, and were invaluable to me. Thank you, Elisabeth—I loved every part of working on this book.

A special mention is needed for Veronica Chambers, who not only steered me to a friendship with Elisabeth, but was the first person in whom I confided about this project. She guided me through my initial fears and helped me in immeasurable ways throughout its creation. I am forever grateful to her.

A huge thanks must be given to the writers who contributed to this book: the phenomenal women—Rebecca Traister, Natalia Sylvester, Jennine Capó Crucet, Carmen Rita Wong, Wendy Carillo, Tracey Ross, Mariana Atencio, MC González Noguera, Erin Aubry Kaplan, Elizabeth Yeampierre, and Prisca Dorcas Mojica Rodríguez—and to our three men! Pedro Regalado, Nathan J. Robinson, and Keegan-Michael Key. A special shout-out goes to Andrea González-Ramírez, who did a deep dive to report out the facts and the story of AOC's life, and gave us the "nuts and bolts" chapter about AOC that made the book complete. And my unending gratitude goes to Patricia Reynoso, my incredibly supportive editor from my *Glam Belleza Latina* days, who not only contributed an essay filled with her beautiful, evocative writing, but supported me and cheered me on and encouraged me with ideas when I needed it most. Thank you, too, to the team at St. Martin's Press— Elisabeth, Alan Bradshaw, Jennifer Simington, Martin Quinn, Sarah Schoof, and Alex Brown.

If not for my family, I would not be the woman that I

am, proud to walk through the world in this Latina skin, and I am unendingly grateful to them; especially to my mother, Guadalupe, who is an entire force of nature, and who along with my dad raised us to believe nothing was impossible; and to my sister, Jennifer. You had more to do with making this book possible than you will ever know. I love you so much and I'm so proud of you.

The last and biggest thanks goes to my little girl, though not so little anymore. The only child of a single mother, Lucie had to endure hours of her mom's nose buried in a laptop, and she was my wonderful and helpful and independent girl all the way through to the end of it. You are truly the reason I do anything. Mommy loves you to the whole world and back.

Notes

INTRODUCTION

1. Office of the NY State Comptroller, "An Economic Snapshot of the Bronx," July 2018. https://www.osc.state.ny.us/osdc/rpt4-2019.pdf.

2. Association of Puerto Rican Executive Directors, "A Call to Action: Puerto Rican New Yorkers," 1985, https://books.google.com/books/about/A_Call_to_Action.html?id=EZQMAAAAYAAJ.

WOMEN LIKE ME AREN'T SUPPOSED TO RUN FOR OFFICE

1. Andrea González-Ramírez, "Meet the Bronx-Born Puerto Rican Challenging One of the Most Powerful House Democrats," Refinery29, June 13, 2018.

2. "New York's 14th Congressional District," Ballotpedia, https://ballotpedia.org/New_York%27s_14th_Congressional_District.

3. Charlotte Alter, "'Change Is Closer Than We Think.' Inside Alexandria Ocasio-Cortez's Unlikely Rise," *Time*, March 21, 2019.

4. Jose Lambiet, "EXCLUSIVE: 'God Played Quite a Joke on Me with This Politics Stuff!' The Privacy-Loving Mother of Alexandria Ocasio-Cortez Whips Up Lasagna as She Tells How She Had to Flee New York Because of High Taxes and Gushes About Wedding Bells for Her Daughter," *Daily Mail*, March 2, 2019.

5. Andy Newman, Vivian Wang, and Luis Ferré-Sadurní, "Alexandria Ocasio-Cortez Emerges as a Political Star," *New York Times,* June 27, 2018.

6. "Portrait of: Alexandria Ocasio-Cortez," *Latino USA,* October 26, 2018; on Bronx and poverty line, see "Focus on Poverty in New York City," New York University Furman Center, June 7, 2017.

7. Maria Newman, "Graduation Rate Declines to Lowest in Eight Years," *New York Times,* December 30, 1994.

8. Alter, "'Change Is Closer Than We Think.'"

9. David Remnick, "Alexandria Ocasio-Cortez's Historic Win and the Future of the Democratic Party," *New Yorker,* July 16, 2018.

10. Wendy Li, "Intel ISEF alumna headed to Capitol Hill," Society for Science & the Public, November 7, 2018, https://www.societyforscience.org/blog/intel-isef-alumna-headed-to-capitol-hill/.

11. 23238 Ocasio-Cortez (2000 WU111), JPL Small-Body Database Browser.

12. Newman, Wang, and Ferré-Sadurní, "Alexandria Ocasio-Cortez Emerges as a Political Star."

13. "Portrait of: Alexandria Ocasio-Cortez."

14. *Knock Down the House,* directed by Rachel Lears, New York: Jubilee Films, Atlas Films, Artemis Rising, 2019.

15. United States Census Bureau, 2010.

16. "Portrait of: Alexandria Ocasio-Cortez."

17. Lambiet, "EXCLUSIVE: 'God Played Quite a Joke on Me with This Politics Stuff!'"

18. Anna Gorman, "Cancer Complications: Confusing Bills, Maddening Errors and Endless Phone Calls," NPR, February 26, 2019.

19. House Oversight and Reform Committee Hearing on Prescription Drug Prices, C-SPAN, July 26, 2019.

20. Remnick, "Alexandria Ocasio-Cortez's Historic Win and the Future of the Democratic Party."

21. Alexandria Ocasio-Cortez (@AOC), Twitter post, September 8, 2018.

22. Remnick, "Alexandria Ocasio-Cortez's Historic Win and the Future of the Democratic Party."

23. Eliza Relman, "The Truth About Alexandria Ocasio-Cortez: The Inside Story of How, in Just One Year, Sandy the Bartender Became a Lawmaker Who Triggers Both Parties," Insider, January 6, 2019; Newman, Wang, and Ferré-Sadurní, "Alexandria Ocasio-Cortez Emerges as a Political Star."

24. Irina Aleksander, "How Alexandria Ocasio-Cortez and Other Progressives Are Defining the Midterms," Vogue, October 15, 2018.

25. Dan Evon, "Did U.S. Rep. Ocasio-Cortez Graduate Cum Laude from Boston University?" Snopes, April 3, 2019.

26. Lambiet, "EXCLUSIVE: 'God Played Quite a Joke on Me with This Politics Stuff!'"

27. Aída Chávez and Ryan Grim, "A Primary Against the Machine: A Bronx Activist Looks to Dethrone Joseph Crowley, the King of Queens," The Intercept, May 22, 2018.

28. Daniel Beekman, "Diverse Group of Startups Thriving at City-Sponsored Sunshine Bronx Business Incubator in Hunts Point," New York Daily News, July 17, 2012.

29. Alter, "'Change Is Closer Than We Think.'"

30. Andrea González-Ramírez, "AOC Goes Back to Her Bartending Roots—for a Good Cause," Refinery29, May 31, 2019.

31. Chas Danner, "Ocasio-Cortez Credits Sanders for Her Political

Awakening at Bernie's Comeback Rally in Queens," *Intelligencer*, October 19, 2019.

32. "Portrait of: Alexandria Ocasio-Cortez."

33. Alter, "'Change Is Closer Than We Think.'"

34. Merrit Kennedy, "Lead-Laced Water in Flint: A Step-by-Step Look at the Makings of a Crisis," NPR, April 20, 2016.

35. Rebecca Solnit, "Standing Rock Inspired Ocasio-Cortez to Run. That's the Power of Protest," *The Guardian*, January 14, 2019.

36. Meagan Day, "Democratic Socialism, Explained by a Democratic Socialist," *Vox*, August 1, 2018.

37. Carl Campanile, "Queens Democratic Party Boss Lives in Northern Virginia," *New York Post*, July 8, 2011.

38. "New York District 14, 2018 Race," OpenSecrets.

39. Christina Maxouris and Saeed Ahmed, "Alexandria Ocasio-Cortez's Campaign Shoes to Join Museum Exhibition," CNN, November 22, 2018.

40. Stephen R. Groves, "Behind Ocasio-Cortez's Upset Victory, an Unconventional Crew," Associated Press, July 7, 2018.

41. Alexandria Ocasio-Cortez (@Ocasio2018), Instagram post, April 13, 2018.

42. Remnick, "Alexandria Ocasio-Cortez's Historic Win and the Future of the Democratic Party."

43. Ryan C. Brooks, "Alexandria Ocasio-Cortez Is Trying to Unseat 'The King of Queens' and Net the First Major Win for the Anti-Establishment Left," *BuzzFeed News*, June 25, 2018.

44. Alexandria Ocasio-Cortez, "The Courage to Change," YouTube, May 30, 2018.

45. Ryan Kelly, "Senior Class: Members of Congress Getting Older," *Roll Call*, October 30, 2017.

46. David Johnson, "These Are the Youngest States in America," *Time*, November 3, 2017.

47. Philip Bump, "70 Percent of White Men in the U.S. Are Represented by a White Man in the House," *Washington Post*, January 12, 2017.

48. United States Census Bureau; "2018 Population Distribution by Race/Ethnicity," Kaiser Family Foundation.

49. Dan Kopf, "The Typical US Congress Member Is 12 Times Richer Than the Typical American Household," *Quartz*, February 12, 2018.

50. Remnick, "Alexandria Ocasio-Cortez's Historic Win and the Future of the Democratic Party."

51. Rebecca C. Lewis, "Crowley Sends 'Worst NYC Lawmaker' to Debate in His Place," City & State: New York, June 19, 2018; Francisco Moya (@FranciscoMoyaNY), Twitter post, June 18, 2018.

52. Alexandria Ocasio-Cortez (@AOC), Twitter post, June 19, 2018.

53. The Editorial Board, "If You Want to Be Speaker, Mr. Crowley, Don't Take Voters for Granted," *New York Times*, June 19, 2018.

54. *Knock Down the House.*

55. Spectrum News NY1 (@NY1), Twitter post, June 26, 2018.

56. Alexi McCammond, "Alexandria Ocasio-Cortez's 2018 Midterms Endorsement List," Axios, July 24, 2018.

57. Laura Nahmias, "'You Can Beat the Establishment': Ocasio-Cortez Crashes Democratic Primaries," *Politico*, July 5, 2018.

58. On clothes, see Megan Garber, "How Alexandria Ocasio-Cortez's Plain Black Jacket Became a Controversy," *The Atlantic*, November 16, 2018; on home, see Gabriella Paiella, "Critic Tries to Discredit

Alexandria Ocasio-Cortez for . . . Living in a House as a Child," *The Cut*, July 2, 2018; on bank account, see Megan Leonhardt, "Alexandria Ocasio-Cortez, the Youngest Woman Ever Elected to Congress, Is Down to Less Than $7,000 in Savings," CNBC, November 16, 2018.

59. Felicia Sonmez, "Ocasio-Cortez Rallies Protesters at Pelosi's Office, Expresses Admiration for Leader," *Washington Post*, November 13, 2018.

60. Nancy Pelosi (@NancyPelosi), Twitter post, November 13, 2018.

61. Jeff Stein, "At Harvard Orientation for Freshman Lawmakers, Skeptical Democrats Confront Lobbyists and CEOs," *Washington Post*, December 7, 2018.

62. Manu Raju, "McCaskill Warns Dems About 'Cheap' Rhetoric; Says GOP Senators Privately Believe Trump Is 'Nuts,'" CNN, January 2, 2019.

63. Elaine Godfrey, "House Democrats Don't Know What to Make of Alexandria Ocasio-Cortez," *The Atlantic*, November 21, 2018.

64. Azi Paybarah, "Alexandria Ocasio-Cortez Will Push Washington. Will Washington Push Back?" *New York Times*, November 7, 2018.

65. Andrea González-Ramírez, "How Alexandria Ocasio-Cortez's Obsession-Worthy Instagram Is Changing the Game," Refinery29, April 17, 2019; Addy Baird, "Inspired by AOC, a Young Progressive Woman Is Trying to Take Down the Second Most Powerful Democrat in the House," *BuzzFeed News*, June 6, 2019.

66. Alexandria Ocasio-Cortez (@ocasio2018), Instagram post, January 5, 2019.

67. Andrea González-Ramírez, "AOC Introduces Ambitious Green New Deal Resolution to Fight Climate Change," Refinery29, February 7, 2019.

68. "Bills Sponsored by Alexandria Ocasio-Cortez (D-N.Y.)," Pro-Publica, August 2015.

69. Sam Wolfson, "Why Ocasio-Cortez's Lesson in Dark Money Is the Most-Watched Political Video," *The Guardian*, February 14, 2019; Emily Kopp, "Ocasio-Cortez Grills CEO of Pharma Company Making Billions on Government-Patented HIV Drug," *Roll Call*, May 16, 2019.

70. Andrea González-Ramírez, "The Freshman Congresswomen Did Their Damn Job at Cohen's Hearing," Refinery29, February 28, 2019.

71. Andrea González-Ramírez, "Why the Progressive Freshman Congresswomen Call Themselves 'The Squad,'" Refinery29, July 16, 2019.

72. Tara Golshan and Ella Nilsen, "Alexandria Ocasio-Cortez's Rocky Rollout of the Green New Deal, Explained," *Vox*, February 11, 2019.

73. Ellen Moynihan and Michael Gartland, "Ocasio-Cortez Opens New Queens District Office, Revisits Amazon Issue," *New York Daily News*, March 4, 2019.

74. Akela Lacy, "Alexandria Ocasio-Cortez's Chief of Staff and Communications Will Depart Her Office," *The Intercept*, August 2, 2019.

75. Bridget Read, "36 Hours with Alexandria Ocasio-Cortez," *Vogue*, June 26, 2019.

76. Martin Pengelly, "'Go Back Home': Trump Aims Racist Attack at Ocasio-Cortez and Other Congresswomen," *The Guardian*, July 15, 2019.

77. Alter, "'Change Is Closer Than We Think.'"

THE DEMOCRATIC SOCIALISM OF AOC

1. Morgan Gstalter, "7 in 10 Millennials Say They Would Vote for a Socialist: Poll," *The Hill*, October 28, 2019, https://thehill.com

/homenews/campaign/467684-70-percent-of-millennials-say
-theyd-vote-for-a-socialist-poll.

2. David Greenberg, "Socialists Are No Strangers to Congress," *Wall Street Journal*, January 3, 2019, https://www.wsj.com/articles /socialists-are-no-strangers-to-congress-11546530927.

3. Nathan Robinson, "Three Arguments Against Socialism and Why They Fail," *Current Affairs*, July 6, 2018, https://www.currentaffairs .org/2018/07/3-arguments-against-socialism-and-why-they-fail.

4. Peter Dreier, "Why Has Milwaukee Forgotten Victor Berger?" *HuffPost*, May 6, 2012, https://www.huffpost.com/entry/why -has-milwaukee-forgott_b_1491463.

5. Chávez and Grim, "A Primary Against the Machine," *The Intercept*, May 22, 2018.

6. See, for example, Rand Paul's *The Case Against Socialism*.

7. Jake Johnson, "Ocasio-Cortez Demands Solar Company Rehire Workers Fired After Unionizing with Green New Deal in Mind," Common Dreams, November 23, 2019, https://www.common dreams.org/news/2019/11/23/ocasio-cortez-demands-solar -company-rehire-workers-fired-after-unionizing-green-new.

8. Josh Eidelson, "Rep. Ocasio-Cortez Criticizes Barstool Sports Founder for Anti-Union Tweets," *Time*, August 14, 2019, https://time .com/5651569/alexandria-ocasio-cortez-barstool-sports-dave- portnoy-anti-union/.

9. "Recognizing the Duty of the Federal Government to Create a Green New Deal," https://ocasio-cortez.house.gov/sites/ocasio- cortez.house.gov/files/Resolution%20on%20a%20Green%20 New%20Deal.pdf.

10. Matthew Walters and Lawrence Mishel, "How Unions Help All Workers," Economic Policy Institute, August 26, 2003, https:// www.epi.org/publication/briefingpapers_bp143/.

11. For "workplace democracy," see https://berniesanders.com/en /issues/workplace-democracy/; for "corporate accountability and democracy," see https://berniesanders.com/issues/corporate -accountability-and-democracy/.

12. For an explanation of why "right-to-work" laws do not expand rights, see Nathan Robinson, "How Expanding the Right to Contract Can Limit Rights," *Current Affairs*, May 23, 2018, https://www .currentaffairs.org/2018/05/why-expansions-of-the-right-to-contract-are-limitations-on-rights.

13. Matthew Yglesias, "Elizabeth Warren Has a Plan to Save Capitalism," *Vox*, August 15, 2018, https://www.vox.com/2018/8/15/17683022 /elizabeth-warren-accountable-capitalism-corporations.

14. Shane Croucher, "How Alexandria Ocasio-Cortez Explains Socialism During Instagram Live Stream," *Newsweek*, June 18, 2019, https://www.newsweek.com/ocasio-cortez-instagram-live -explains-socialism-aoc-1444534.

15. Alexandria Ocasio-Cortez (@AOC), Twitter, October 7, 2019, 6:58 a.m., https://twitter.com/AOC/status/1181207065072676864.

16. Sheryl Gay Stolberg, "Ocasio-Cortez Calls Migrant Detention Centers 'Concentration Camps,' Eliciting Backlash," *New York Times*, June 18, 2019, https://www.nytimes.com/2019/06/18/us /politics/ocasio-cortez-cheney-detention-centers.html.

17. Carimin Chappell, "Alexandria Ocasio-Cortez: A System That Allows Billionaires to Exist Alongside Extreme Poverty Is Immoral," CNBC, January 22, 2019, https://www.cnbc.com/2019/01/22 /alexandria-ocasio-cortez-a-system-that-allows-billionaires-to-exist-is-immoral.html.

18. "A Just Society," https://ocasio-cortez.house.gov/ajs.

19. Danielle Kurtzleben, "Rep. Alexandria Ocasio-Cortez Releases Green New Deal Outline," NPR, February 7, 2019, https://www

.npr.org/2019/02/07/691997301/rep-alexandria-ocasio-cortez
-releases-green-new-deal-outline.

20. Chris Cillizza, "129 Seconds That Perfectly Explain Why Liberals Go Wild for Alexandira Ocasio-Cortez," KSL NewsRadio, March 27, 2019, https://kslnewsradio.com/1903178/129-seconds-perfectly-explain-liberals-go-wild-alexandria-ocasio-cortez/?.

21. Ryan Grim and Briahna Gray, "Alexandria Ocasio-Cortez Joins Environmental Activists in Protest at Democratic Leader Nancy Pelosi's Office," *The Intercept*, November 13, 2018, https://theinter cept.com/2018/11/13/alexandria-ocasio-cortez-sunrise-activists -nancy-pelosi/.

22. Akela Lacy, "House Democratic Leadership Warns It Will Cut Off Any Firms That Challenge Incumbents," *The Intercept*, March 22, 2019, https://theintercept.com/2019/03/22/house-democratic-leadership -warns-it-will-cut-off-any-firms-who-challenge-incumbents/.

23. Chávez and Grim, "A Primary Against The Machine."

24. Alexandria Ocasio-Cortez (@AOC), Twitter, February 22, 2019, 6:27 p.m., https://twitter.com/aoc/status/1099133711986163713?s=21.

25. Alexandria Ocasio-Cortez (@AOC), Twitter, March 12, 2019, 1:00 p.m., https://twitter.com/cspan/status/1105559308211798020.

26. On Amazon, see Alexandria Ocasio-Cortez (@AOC), Twitter, February 15, 7:36 a.m., https://twitter.com/aoc/status/109643307 8136901634?s=21; on support for workers, see Alexandria Ocasio-Cortez (@AOC), Twitter, June 25, 2019, 11:45 a.m., https://twitter. com/aoc/status/1143590995122171905?s=21.

27. Alexandria Ocasio-Cortez (@AOC), Twitter, January 23, 2019, 6:20 p.m., https://twitter.com/AOC/status/1088260329610625024.

28. On lobbyist project, see Sinéad Baker, "Alexandria Ocasio-Cortez Slams Harvard Orientation for Freshman Lawmakers as 'Lobbyist

Project' That Hypes Tax Cuts for Corporations," *Business Insider*, December 10, 2018, https://www.businessinsider.com/alexandria-ocasio-cortez-harvard-house-orientation-lobbyists-2018-12; on homeless people, see Alexandria Ocasio-Cortez (@AOC), Twitter, February 13, 2019, 11:16 a.m., https://twitter.com/AOC/status/1095763596062150656.

29. Lee Moran, "Alexandria Ocasio-Cortez Reveals How Many F**ks She Gives After Colbert Asks," *HuffPost*, January 22, 2019, https://www.huffpost.com/entry/alexandria-ocasio-cortez-stephen-colbert-zero_n_5c471158e4b0a8dbe174f171.

30. Chantal Da Silva, "Ocasio-Cortez Slams Israeli 'Occupation,' Walks It Back: I Am 'Not The Expert'," *Newsweek*, July 18, 2018, https://www.newsweek.com/ocasio-cortez-slams-israeli-occupation-walks-it-back-i-am-not-expert-1029386.

31. Daniel Strauss, "Ocasio-Cortez and Sanders Work to Elect First Muslim Governor," *Politico*, August 4, 2018, https://www.politico.com/story/2018/08/04/michigan-governor-el-sayed-ocasio-cortez-sanders-democrats-762409.

32. On dancing outside her office, see https://www.youtube.com/watch?v=ZBeuzWWKrew; on having fun with a penguin, see Alexandria Ocasio-Cortez (@AOC), Twitter, August 24, 2019, 12:09 p.m., https://twitter.com/aoc/status/1165340309384908800?lang=en; on getting licked by a dog, see https://www.youtube.com/watch?v=c-bQFq2yGYNI.

ON BEING AN INDIGNANT BROWN GIRL

1. Ronald W. Reagan, "Executive Orders," *National Archives and Records Administration*, National Archives and Records Administration, www.archives.gov/federal-register/codification/executive-order/12513.html.

MAKING THE GREEN NEW DEAL THE REAL DEAL

1. Climate Justice Alliance, "A Green New Deal Must Be Rooted in a Just Transition for Workers and Communities Most Impacted by Climate Change," press release, December 10, 2018, https:// climatejusticealliance.org/green-new-deal-must-rooted-just -transition-workers-communities-impacted-climate-change/.